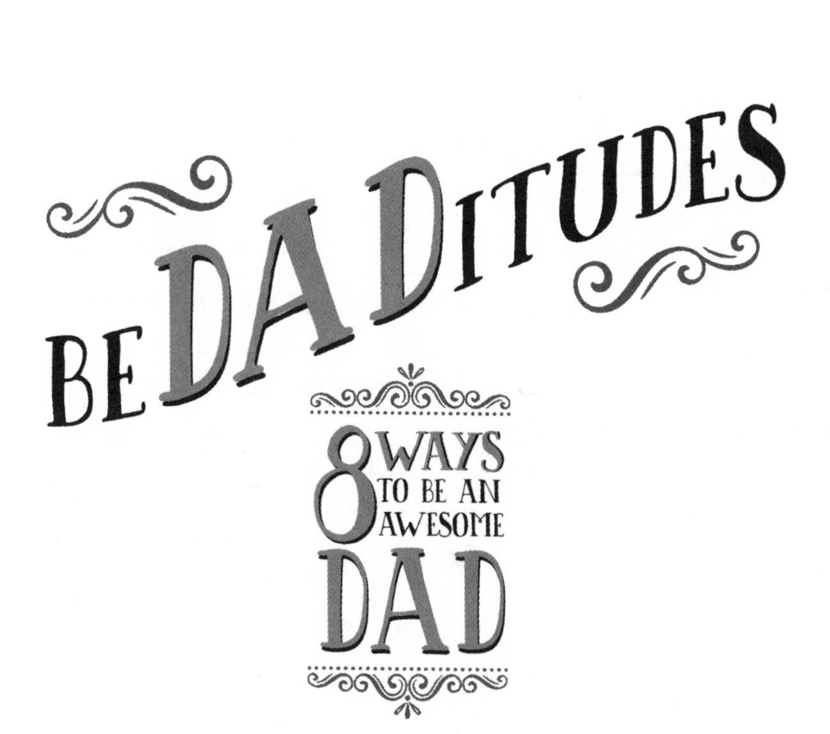
BeDADitudes
8 Ways to Be an Awesome Dad

"Greg Popcak gives the modern dad an invaluable gift. In clear and practical terms, Popcak creates not only a vision for being a successful father but a strategy to get there. His examples are relevant and plausible, and the results will be seen almost immediately in the lives of dads everywhere. In a culture that is suffering from a pandemic of fatherlessness, both physically and emotionally, *BeDADitudes* is an antidote that will not only change families but, ultimately, save souls."

**Mark Hart**
Catholic author, speaker, radio host, and
executive vice president at Life Teen International

"Greg Popcak delves into Jesus' teachings found in the Sermon on the Mount and pulls out powerful, life-changing ideas for dads that will help them influence their families and change our world."

**John Bergsma**
Author of *Bible Basics for Catholics*

"Our culture often distorts how men should relate to their wives and children. *BeDADitudes* seeks to fix that misshapen image with the beauty of Catholic wisdom. Insightful, practical, and balanced, Greg Popcak gets at the heart of what men think and feel, busting the myths and charting a path to authentic Catholic fatherhood. Highly recommended for any man seeking to be a better dad and lead his family closer to God."

**Marc Cardaronella**
Author of *Keep Your Kids Catholic*

"Our culture is in the midst of a great crisis of fatherhood resulting in devastating consequences. We need a resurrection of authentic Christian fathers. In *BeDADitudes*, Gregory Popcak issues a compassionate and convicted call to return to the fatherhood found in the heart of God. Using the eight Beatitudes found in the gospels, Popcak outlines the character of authentic fatherhood, and teaches us that we can't learn to be good fathers until we've learned to be good sons. With humor, insight, and an accessible style, he answers common misconceptions and challenges men to embrace the greatness of being a vocational dad. I highly recommend this book."

**Sam Guzman**
Founder of *The Catholic Gentleman*

GREGORY K. POPCAK

Ave Maria Press AVE Notre Dame, Indiana

Founded in 1865, Ave Maria Press is a ministry of the United States Province of Holy Cross.

www.avemariapress.com

Paperback: ISBN-13 978-1-59471-718-5

E-book: ISBN-13 978-1-59471-719-2

Cover image © iStockphoto.

Cover and text design by Christopher D. Tobin.

Printed and bound in the United States of America.

*Library of Congress Cataloging-in-Publication Data is available.*

# CONTENTS

# INTRODUCTION

## Striving for Greatness

God wants to make you a father after his own heart! Wherever you came from, whatever your history, whatever you think of your present abilities, whatever your current state in life, God has a plan to transform you into the father you are meant to be through his love and grace.

There are many different ideas about what it takes to be a great father, and some of those different models can contradict one another. In a world where even the words "marriage" and "family" mean radically different things to different people, men are more confused than ever about what it means to be a father, much less a godly father. In this troubled age, a Christian father must have more to rely upon than the example of his own father or culture. Instead, the Christian father must take as his model the blueprint Christ himself drew in the Sermon on the Mount when he gave us the eight Beatitudes, those key principles that distinguish the Christian worldview from all others. The eight Beatitudes are the provocative standard by which we measure every other vision of what fatherhood entails. They are the standard by which the example of our own fathers or the culture's idea of fatherhood or our own efforts at fathering must stand or fall.

## Pursuing the Fullness of Fatherhood

The word *beatitude* means "a state of utmost fulfillment." The Beatitudes represent the path we walk toward sainthood. We Christians are on a journey that leads us to our total fulfillment, to becoming everything that God created us to be in this life, and, ultimately, to spending eternity in heaven with him in the next. We can think of the eight Beatitudes as the paving stones Jesus lays before us that enable us to walk the path that leads to our destiny in Christ and unites us with our heavenly Father. Every time we follow the mission expressed in one of the Beatitudes, we take one more step toward conforming ourselves to the image of Christ and being witnesses to our Father's love. In fact, Pope Francis asserted that the Beatitudes are the "identity card of a Christian" and a "program" for living every aspect of the Christian life.

When we practice the Beatitudes in our fathering efforts, we seek to attain the utmost fullness of fatherhood by striving to become transparent, so that when our wives and children look at us, they see God's own loving face looking back at them. To borrow the words of John the Baptist, "He must increase; I must decrease" (Jn 3:30). Our ministry as fathers is only effective to the degree that we reveal the face of God to our wives and children in our words and actions. The Beatitudes are power-packed principles that show us how to make this a reality in every aspect of our lives, especially our fatherhood.

## The BeDADitudes

As key as these eight blessings are to the Christian life in general, we don't often think of them as a blueprint for Christian fatherhood. I think that's a serious mistake. St. John Paul II's theology of the body teaches that masculinity finds its fullest expression in spiritual and biological fatherhood and that all Christian men must draw close to their fatherly identity to be true reflections of God the Father, in whose image we are made.

The eight Beatitudes define the nature of God the Father's relationship with his children, and they present a model for the heart of Christian fatherhood. God's very own poverty in spirit allowed him to empty himself and become a slave that his children might be set free. God the Father's willingness to mourn for his hurting children allows us to receive his abundant providence and mercy. His own thirst for righteousness compels him to seek the restoration of a world fallen from grace and the salvation of the very children who have turned their backs on him. God the Father's own purity of heart compels him to want to make us pure and spotless that we might live with him forever. And so on. Each of the Beatitudes Jesus enumerated in his Sermon on the Mount reveals God the Father's love for us, teaches us how we might conform our hearts to his, and invites us as disciples to live out these same principles in our relationships with our own children.

Expressed through our fatherhood, the eight blessings Jesus proclaimed on Mount Eremos by the Sea of Galilee become the eight BeDADitudes, each of which can help any man become the father God means him to be—a father after God's own heart. Because fatherhood is a ministry that is both rooted in our divine sonship and is the fruit of our ministry as husbands, each chapter will look at how each BeDADitude orders our relationships across three dimensions: our relationships with God, our relationships with our wives, and our relationships with our children.

## Blessed Are You!

Being a father is tough work, but I am convinced that there is no more valuable and blessed role you can play or work you can do. You have been given true power by virtue of the office of your fatherhood to make a real difference in the lives of your spouse and children and, through your witness of heroic virtue in your family life, to lead the world to Christ. Throughout this book, you will discover how to both rejoice in your role as father and experience the graces of fatherhood on a deeper level. You will be the "man after [God's] own heart" (see Acts 13:22) who is empowered by God's grace to create a revolution of the family that will both fill your home with the love of God and call the world to Christ through the light that shines out of the heart of your household.

This book is for every father who wants to learn what it takes to claim both his family and the world for Christ. It is for every father who wants to find the courage to prove that godly men are a people set apart. Called to be grace-filled heroes, masters of our own passions and defenders of those who depend upon us, much will be required of us if we choose this path, but much will be given to us as well. Those who take up the challenge of faithful fatherhood presented by each of the eight BeDADitudes will receive the grace to transform their families into jewels in God's crown. If you are ready to discover what it takes to be the kind of father that can lead that kind of family, keep reading.

# THE FIRST BEDADITUDE

## Blessed are the dads who are poor in spirit. Theirs is the kingdom of heaven!

What does it mean to be "poor in spirit"?

According to scripture scholars, the man who is poor in spirit is profoundly aware of his radical dependence on God. Men often struggle with this idea. Many of us have been raised to believe that it is a virtue to be self-sufficient. Boys are taught from toddlerhood that they are "sissies" if they need their mothers or fathers "too much." The world tells us, "Blessed is the man who takes care of himself and minds his own affairs."

But this attitude is completely contrary to the message of Jesus. In the words of Pope Francis, "When the heart is rich and self-satisfied, it has no place for the Word of God."[1] The man who would follow Jesus and model his heart after that of the Father's must reject this idea and embrace the humility that allows him, his son, to follow in his footsteps.

### *You Are a Communion*

Jesus' admonition to embrace poverty in spirit flies in the face of the rugged individualism that most of us have been taught to see as the height of masculinity. Through the Beatitudes, Jesus radically reconfigures our idea of what it means to be a man. Instead of conforming ourselves to the worldly vision of a solitary man living life on his own terms, Jesus reminds us that we are made in the image and likeness of God, who is, in his very being, a communion of persons. Even "on his own," so to speak, God the Father *is* communion. We cannot know the Father without also simultaneously encountering the Son and the Holy Spirit.

So what? Well, the Christian understanding of masculinity means that a man must always simultaneously carry his roles of son, husband, and father before him. If he is to set himself on the path to fulfilling his masculine identity, even the so-called "single man" must live with his future husbandhood and fatherhood in mind. Doesn't the one-night stand the single man has today cheat his future wife of the single-minded devotion that is deservedly hers? Doesn't the single man who pours himself entirely into his work today make it that much harder to be present to his future children? We are never our own, and we must never live as if we are. Our bodies, our very selves, belong to God first, then to the wives God desires for us, and then to the children (actual and/or spiritual) that God intends to give us. The young man who has lived for himself as a teen and young adult and imagines that marriage and family life means that it is time to "settle down" has been living an illusion of masculinity. He has no idea what it is fulfills his true identity as a man. In fact, he has been living as little more than an animal. Same with the workaholic man who neglects his wife and children. How is he more enlightened than any other beast of burden, applying himself to the task at hand without any mind to his greater significance and purpose? Such a "man" might accomplish much in his life, but it profits him nothing, for he has lost his true identity even before he ever found it (see Mk 8:36).

God wants to set us free from these false visions of masculinity, from these traps that Satan uses to makes us settle for less than what we truly are—men of God! Christian tradition teaches us that man does not begin to live until he lives for others (cf. *Gaudium et Spes*) and, more specifically, until he begins to live for the wife who is his helpmate and the children their love brings into the world. This threefold identity helps keep the Christian man anchored in his identity in Christ. Let's look at how cultivating this poverty of spirit, first in our own relationships with God, then in our relationships with our spouses, and finally in our relationships with our children, can help us take giant steps toward becoming the kind of men God intends us to be.

## *Blessed Are the Dads Who Are Poor in Spirit*

### Your Relationship with God

We are sons of God, and as his sons we must learn to follow in our Father's footsteps. God wants to set us free to be the men we were created to be, men after his very own heart, but to experience this freedom we first have to turn to God—every single day—and face three life-changing truths:

1. I do not know what I am doing, and I cannot fulfill my destiny and lead my family on my own.
2. God loves me unconditionally and wants to make me whole.
3. God will lead me if I turn to him first.

#### *1. I do not know what I am doing, and I cannot fulfill my destiny and lead my family on my own.*

Men in general, and fathers in particular, put a tremendous amount of pressure on themselves. We know we are meant to lead our wives and our children to God; however, many of us were not raised in homes where this mission was modeled for us. Even if we were, our own families might be radically different than our families of origin. We intuitively know that we don't have the first idea of how to become the men God calls us to be or how to lead our families to Christ, and it often terrifies us.

Rather than embracing this ignorance in humility and asking God to teach us what to do, we often pretend we know. We try to cover our ignorance and the fear of our incompetence by setting ourselves up as the angry, part-time pagan deities of our households. We make unilateral dictates and bluster and rage about petty slights to our "authority" and "headship." But if we fall prey to this temptation, any rebellion we experience on the part of our wives or children is not defiance against us. It is actually obedience to the impulse God has created in every one of his children to resist bowing down to any god but him (see Ex 20:3).

In order to lead authentically, our wives and children must see that we are trying to walk in our Father's footsteps. They must see us acknowledging our ignorance—after all, they already know we don't know what we're doing—and asking our Father for guidance. The father who is poor in spirit knows that he is strongest when he is on his knees with his face turned to God. As St. Paul reminds us, we are strongest when we acknowledge our weakness (see 2 Cor 12:10).

## Questions for Reflection

- When are you tempted to pretend to be more competent than you are?
- Are there times you set yourself as the god of your household instead of making God himself the head of your house?
- Do you admit your weakness and confusion about life to God? How have you experienced God's response to your humility?

### *2. God loves me unconditionally and wants to make me whole.*

Philosophers, theologians, and even psychologists tell us that to love someone is to will and work for that person's good. To say, "I love you," is a shorthand way of promising, "I want to do everything I can to help you become everything you were meant to be." To say, "I love you . . . unconditionally," is to say, "I will always do everything I can to help you become everything you were meant to be whether I feel like it or not, whether I feel that you deserve it or not, and whether it is easy or not."

This is how God loves you. He wants to make you perfect, as your heavenly Father is perfect. That might sound oppressive at first, and it would be if we were left on our own to figure it out. But God's plan for our perfection is even more ambitious than that. He doesn't leave us on our own to figure it out. He works right alongside us. He'll even make it happen in us if we let him. Whatever you think stops you from being the best and godliest husband or father you can be, God wants to remove and heal you. Yes, you will have to ask him into your heart and you will have to cooperate with the grace he gives you, but this is the difference between shoveling the driveway on your own power versus using a snowblower. Both can be challenging in their own ways, but the latter is infinitely easier and even enjoyable. God loves you unconditionally and wants to make you whole. You don't have to pretend to know everything. You don't have to kill yourself to make it all work on your own power. You just have to turn to God in your weakness, ask him to burrow deeper into your heart every day, and allow him to transform you from the inside out.

## Questions for Reflection

- How have you experienced God's grace helping you overcome your weaknesses and imperfections?
- Describe the difference between times you have tried to lean harder on God's grace versus times you tried to do something by yourself.

### *3. God will lead me if I turn to him first.*

"Just tell me what to do." I hear this from men in counseling all the time. We approach our prayer lives the same way. We don't want true internal conversion. We just want God to give us our marching orders so that we can run off and make the world—and our families—right for him. As well-intentioned as this sounds, can you hear the pride in it? "Just tell *me* what to do, and *I* will make *the world* and *my family* right for God." As if we could do anything for him on our own power. As if we could figure anything out on our own.

If we put the plea, "Just tell me what to do," to God, the answer will always be the same whether we are asking for help with personal struggles, marital challenges, or family problems. God's answer will always be, "Be still and know that I am God" (Ps 46:11). You are not God. God is God. Yes, he wants to lead you. Yes, he wants to transform you from the inside out. But in order for him to take the lead in your life and in your heart and in your house, you must invite him to do it. You must step out of the driver's seat and hand the keys over to him. Being the head of your home doesn't mean you are the leader of your home as much as it means you are the first follower of Jesus Christ, the true head of your household.

God will have mercy on your weakness and brokenness as a man, a husband, and a father. He will work to make you whole, and he will enable you to lead your family to glory. But first you have to stop trying to fix it all yourself. Give yourself the gift of surrendering the need to pretend that you have it all under control. Even if you were the most competent man in the world, you couldn't possibly begin to know, much less consider, all the variables God is aware of and that inform his will for you, your wife, and your children. Before every important decision, before you take any action as a man, husband, or father, let your simple prayer be this:

> Lord, I am trying to do my best. But you and I both know that I don't really know what I'm doing. I ask you to lead me. I ask you to transform my heart and make it like yours. I place myself under your headship. Show me how to be a man after your own heart. Show me how to truly love and lead my wife and family—not out of my will but yours. Give me listening ears and a servant's heart. Help me remember that, to be the head of this family, I must be your first follower.

### Questions for Reflection

- Have you ever admitted your weakness to God? If you have, how did God deal with it? If not, what would enable you to do so?
- Have you ever asked God to heal you of your pride and spirit of self-reliance? What would change if you did?

## *Blessed Are the Dads Who Are Poor in Spirit*

### Your Relationship with Your Wife

Having reconciled yourself to the fact that you are not in control and that God is the head of your house—not you—you are ready to lead your family as the "first follower" in your home. But what does that mean? Being the "first follower" in your home does not grant you psychic or magical powers to know the right thing to do. Rather, it gives you power to invite your wife to kneel down beside you in prayer and give her heart and the heart of your marriage to God.

Remember, pride says, "I am going to fix everything in my life and set my household right for God," but poverty of spirit says, "I know that I don't know how to fix anything on my own, including my household, and so I bring myself and my household to God, who does know how to put everything in right order. Teach us, Lord, your ways."

You cannot be a husband who is poor in spirit if you do not lead couple-prayer in your marriage. You might have the most amazing individual prayer life, but how is it possible to have a godly marriage if you and your wife don't submit yourselves to God in prayer on a daily basis? If you go off and pray by yourself and then tell your wife what you heard, how is that not setting yourself up as some kind of anointed oracle in your home? Yes, it is a good first step, but it is only the first step. Bring your bride to pray with you, and ask God to teach you both how to love. Let her see you humbling yourself before God, and she will give you her heart in ways you never dreamed possible.

Many men find the idea of couple-prayer to be strange if not outright offensive. They think it is "too private" to share even with their wives. The *Catechism* tells us that Christian prayer is never private. It is always communal by nature because it draws us closer into communion with God and all the holy men and women of God who have gone before us. Even when we pray alone, all the saints and angels are praying with us. We are never less alone than when we pray.

In my experience, most men who actively resist couple-prayer (as opposed to embracing it despite some initial discomfort) are actually resistant to the idea that the Christian walk is a call to true internal conversion. They don't want God to change them from the inside out. They just want to be told what to do so they can keep being what they already are. Although they may mean well on some level, these men know that they are merely going through the motions of having spiritual lives, and they prefer not to let their wives see through their shallow efforts to fake God out.

But what if no one ever taught you how to pray as a couple? I'm glad you asked. There is no one right way to pray, of course, as long as you are truly putting your heart into it. You should feel free to pray in whatever manner draws you and your wife closer to God *and* each other. What's that? Are you surprised that praying with your wife should bring you closer to God and your wife? Prayer is first and foremost an intimate activity. It binds us closer to God and the people we are praying with so that we can be one as the Father and Son are one (see Jn 17:21). So by all means, pray in whatever manner accomplishes this for you and your wife. Don't just say words out loud in each other's presence. Share your hearts with God and each other. With that in mind, I would like to recommend a template I call the PRAISE format.

Sit next to your wife. Put your arm around her if you like. Close your eyes. Pause for a breath to clear your mind of all the noise. Then, out loud, say something like, "Lord, we come into your presence and place ourselves in your care. Help us to love you, each other, our children, and all those you place in our path with your love." Use your own words. Speak from the heart. Then, if you like, walk through the steps of PRAISE.

## *P: Praise and Thanksgiving*

Each of you should take a moment to praise God for what he means to you and how you are experiencing him in your life (for example, "Lord, I praise you for your mercy and kindness. I praise you for your providence and generosity. I praise your for your love."). When we praise God, we tell him what he means to us.

Then take a moment to thank God for the particular blessings of the day. Don't forget to thank God for your spouse (for example, "Thank you, God, for letting this wonderful woman share my life."). Use your own words. Think it through. How has God blessed you that day? How is your life better because of the wife and children you have? Thank God for those blessings.

### R: Repent

Now it's time to ask for God's help with your struggles. Don't worry. You don't need to confess your sins to each other. But take some time to ask God for help with the little and obvious ways you may have let him or each other down (what Matthew Kelly calls your "fears, faults and failures" in *The Seven Levels of Intimacy*). For example say this: "Lord, I'm sorry I lost my temper with my kids earlier today. Help me be more patient and understanding." "Lord, I know I tend to get distracted by my work. Help me really listen when my wife is speaking to me."[2] Ask God to help you overcome the little limitations that stop you from being as truly loving to each other and your kids as God would want you to be.

### A: Ask for Your Needs

Next, take a moment to ask God for whatever intentions are on your heart as individuals and as a couple. Let God, and your spouse, know your needs and concerns.

### I: Intercede

Don't forget to pray for those who are in special need of God's grace. Remember to bring your children and their concerns to God at this time as well.

### S: Seek His Will

Beyond the simple prayer requests we might have, we often have bigger questions or concerns that might not be so easily answered. These might be questions about changes we would like to make in our working lives, moves we might like to make, or issues that we're struggling with as couples. Bring it to God, and ask him what he wants you to do (for example, "Lord, we are both really unsure of whether it's time to have another child or not. Help us to really attend to each other's concerns well and to do your will.").

### *E: Express Your Desire to Serve Him until You Meet Again in Prayer*

Now it's time to wrap up. Say something like, "Lord, thank you for this time together. Help us to hear your voice and know your will as we go about our day. We ask this in Jesus' name, amen."

This brief conclusion helps to remind you that prayer doesn't end when you say "amen." It really just begins. "Amen" means "your will be done." It is our way as Christians of promising God that we will be listening for his voice throughout the day. Make sure you keep listening to God after you say "amen."

Some of you might be wondering where formal prayers like the Rosary, the Divine Mercy Chaplet, or even the Divine Office fit in here. The answer is—anywhere you like. Perhaps PRAISE can be the way you lead into these beautiful prayers of the Church. Or perhaps you would wish to conclude with them. However you integrate more formal prayers into your couple-prayer time, just make sure to find a way to bring your hearts and minds to God. Don't just say words together and call it couple-prayer. Find some way to focus your hearts, minds, and desires through whatever prayers you choose. Bring yourselves and your lives together to God honestly, sincerely, and vulnerably. Let him teach you how to be the man and woman he is calling you to be with each other and for each other.

## Questions for Reflection

- What is your experience of couple-prayer? What would it take for you to become comfortable praying together with your wife?
- When would be the best time for you and your wife to have couple-prayer time?

- What blessings do you think couple-prayer could bring to your marriage if you and your wife did it consistently and sincerely?

## Prayer

Heavenly Father, open my heart in joining together with my wife so I can learn to love her as you do. Help me to overcome any fears that would hold me back from sharing my soul as well as my body with my bride. Make me poor in spirit so that I would be willing to share the deepest parts of myself with both you and my beloved, so that you would be able to make my marriage into the miracle of love and grace that it is meant to be. Amen.

# ***Blessed Are the Dads Who Are Poor in Spirit***

## Your Relationship with Your Children

As a father, poverty of spirit means that you recognize that your primary job is introducing your children to their heavenly Father. You must decrease so he will increase (see Jn 3:30). There is no more important thing you can do than to let your children know how much their heavenly Father loves them and cares for them. As Jesus said, "If you then, who are wicked, know how to give good gifts to your children, how much more will your heavenly Father give good things to those who ask him" (Mt 7:11).

Here are some ways you can introduce your children to their heavenly Father:

- Read Bible stories to them at bedtime. Use different voices. Make the stories exciting!
- Give your kids blessings. Lay your hands on their heads and pray over them before they go to school, have practice or a game, or go to bed. Ask God to bless them and to help them discover and use all the talents he has given them for his glory.

- Lead meal and bedtime prayers. Make these times warm and loving.
- Be affectionate, especially at prayer time. Research shows that children who experience the faith as the source of the warmth in their homes are much more likely to own their faith as adults.
- When your kids are hurting—emotionally or physically—pray with them. Help them talk to God about it.
- When your kids have something to celebrate, pray with them. Help them to give God special thanks for this blessing in the moment.
- Help your wife get the kids ready for church. Don't be a task-master. Be calm. Help keep down the emotional temperature in the house. Getting to church on time is important, but if you have to choose between getting to church on time and getting there as a loving family unit, choose the latter.
- Have your own prayer time. Don't make a show of it, but do it at home so your kids know it's happening.
- When you are getting angry or losing patience with your kids, tell them to wait a minute. Ask them to join you in prayer. Hold hands. Ask God out loud to help you be the father they need you to be and to open their hearts to your care and instruction.
- When you're going through a challenging time—physically or emotionally—ask your children to pray over you. Tell them to use their own words. Help them if they get stuck.
- Lead conversations about faith topics. Don't lecture or moralize. Ask questions of your kids, then look up the answers together in the Bible or *Catechism*.
- Encourage your kids to have their own times of prayer—just like you. Help them set up a time when they will take a few moments

with God. Coach them on what that prayer time should look like. If you don't know, teach them the PRAISE format.

## Questions for Reflection

- In what ways did your father help or hinder your relationship with your heavenly Father? Take a moment to pray for your father.
- In what ways do you help your children find their heavenly Father already? What more could you do to encourage your kids to experience the love of their heavenly Father?

In all things, we must remember to model that God is the true head of our households. He is our children's true Father. One day, they will return to him. It is our job as fathers to teach our children how to find their heavenly Father. Jesus does not mince words on this point. It would be better for a father to have a brick tied around his neck and thrown into the sea than for him to do anything that would stop his children from finding their heavenly Father (see Lk 17:2).

But as the first Beatitude teaches us, the father who practices poverty of spirit by placing God first in his life, by going to God with his wife so that God could teach them both how to truly love each other, and by helping his children find their heavenly Father hiding in plain sight in every moment of every day, will inherit the kingdom of heaven. God will use your poverty of spirit to be the engine that transforms your home into a spiritual powerhouse, enabling your family to experience the depths of God's love and to be light to the world of the wonders God can work in his imperfect people when they place him at the center of their lives.

## Prayer

Heavenly Father, teach me to be poor in spirit. Help me to remember that without you I am nothing, but with you I can become a man after your own heart, a man whose love of and service to his family can lead them into true communion with you. Help me be that man. I surrender everything to your holy will. Amen.

# THE SECOND BEDADITUDE

## Blessed are the dads who mourn. They will be comforted.

"Blessed are they who mourn" (Mt 5:4). Understood superficially, I have always had two problems with this Beatitude.

First, mourning seems like a passive thing. Isn't mourning something that occurs naturally in the face of loss or pain? Isn't mourning something that just happens to me? If the Beatitudes are qualities I should cultivate in my life to conform myself to Christ, how do I actively pursue something that is usually considered to be a passive response—and such a miserably passive response at that? It appears to make no sense.

Second, it seems so depressing. Is Jesus really saying that to be like him we need to make ourselves sad all the time? Why? About what exactly? Jesus came that we might have life and have it more abundantly (see Jn 10:10). Is our response to this gift really supposed to be "boo-hoo. Woe is me!"?

Of course not. In fact, both of these difficulties are rooted in a misunderstanding of what it means to mourn. As the Beatitude speaks of it, mourning isn't the same thing as grieving; it's having a deep compassion for the cares and hurts of the people who depend on you. Just as our heavenly Father rushes to meet our needs before they are even on our lips (see Ps 139:4) and aches to heal our hurts, Christian fathers must become deeply empathic to the needs of the people who look to them for care.

Romans 12:15 reminds us to "rejoice with those who rejoice [and] weep with those who weep." We men are often uncomfortable with feelings of sadness, hurt, discomfort, loss, pain, loneliness, or grief in ourselves or others. We are taught that there are only two options in the face of such strong negative emotions: we can power through them (or numb them with drink and drugs), or we can be consumed by them. The same goes for the way we deal with other people's experience of the same feelings. We either get angry at them for burdening us with their negativity, run away and refuse to be around them for fear of catching their negativity, or insist that they try to get over themselves as a condition of sticking around.

Jesus is presenting another option, an option that tells us that we do not have to be afraid of either our own or others' feelings. Jesus wants to share with us the perfect love that casts out all fears (see 1 Jn 4:18), and he wants to empower us to be instruments of that same love in the lives of others. Jesus assures us that if we allow ourselves to be honest with our feelings, to be present to others in their feelings, and to bring all of those feelings to him (instead of trying to deal with them on our own) we can escape the unhealthy opposites of being consumed by misery or living in denial. We can, instead, both mourn with those who mourn and be comforted. Moreover, we can be godly sources of comfort in the lives of others who are sad or in pain. In the words of Pope Francis, "The world tells us that happiness, joy and entertainment are the best things in life. And it looks the other way when there are problems in the family. The world does not want to suffer, it prefers to ignore painful situations, to cover them up. Only the person who sees things as they are, and whose heart mourns, will be happy and will be comforted."[2]

The message of this Beatitude for us fathers is that, because Christ is our strength, we men of God don't have to be afraid of feelings anymore. We can develop the compassion for ourselves and others that is rooted in the love that flows from the very heart of God for his hurting children.

In the following pages, we'll explore how God wants to allow his sons to experience true compassion for themselves, for their wives, and for their children.

## *Blessed Are the Dads Who Mourn*

### Your Relationship with God

Your heavenly Father loves you more than you could possibly know. Your joys are his joys. Your struggles are his struggles. Your sorrows are his sorrows. Cast your cares upon the Lord, and he will sustain you. He will never let the righteous be shaken (see Ps 55:23).

In the last chapter, we spoke of the need for poverty of spirit, the humility that allows us to be comfortable with the idea that we do not have to handle things on our own and that in fact it is not only acceptable but desirable to God that his sons admit their weaknesses so that he can be their strength.

But once we are free to admit our weaknesses, the next step is to have compassion for ourselves. This is a completely alien concept to many, even most, men. We men are often raised to believe that weakness jeopardizes our masculinity. We are told that we cannot be both weak and manly. We are taught that if we must admit that we have imperfections then we are obliged to respond to those imperfections with self-hatred, self-loathing, condemnation, and criticism. What an incredible lie we have been told. In this Beatitude, Jesus wipes away this lie and speaks the truth that sets us free. He tells us that if we can respond to our woundedness with compassion rather than condemnation, we can be healed. Blessed are those who mourn, for they shall be comforted.

Your heavenly Father knows your pain. He knows your imperfections. He knows every last one of your limitations. He does not condemn you for them (see Jn 8:11). He wants to love you for them. And if you let him, he will love you through them. We must learn to cry out to God when we are troubled so that he can deliver us either from ourselves or the troubles that are consuming us. We cannot give what we do not have. Before we can give our wives and children the love of the Father, we have to experience it for ourselves. The following can help you break free of the trap of self-condemnation and begin to experience the healing compassion of your heavenly Father:

1. Confess your pain to God.
2. Master your inner voice.
3. Dwell on his mercy.
4. Accept responsibility.

### *1. Confess your pain to God.*

When we are blessed with the grace to mourn our weaknesses, we are freed from the desire to run away from the grace and healing God wants to give us by denying that there could possibly be anything wrong in our lives. When you are facing your limitations and are struggling, frustrated, hurting, or in pain, bring them immediately to your Father in heaven. When our limitations cause us to sin, this means going to Confession and receiving the forgiveness of God. Yes, we can confess our sins privately to God and receive his forgiveness, but Jesus knew we needed more, so he gave his apostles the power to forgive sins in his name (see Jn 20:23; Mt 16:19, 18:18). When we bring our failings to God in Confession, we receive powerful confirmations that God meets our brokenness with compassion and our woundedness with healing grace.

"I absolve you of all your sins in the name of the Father, and of the Son, and of the Holy Spirit." We may be tempted to indulge in self-condemnation, but our heavenly Father doesn't waste any time on such distractions from his mercy and healing love. Like the Father of the returning prodigal son, in Confession, God runs to meet us on the road, wraps us in his arms, and restores our sonship. We are made new in his loving embrace.

Of course, we also encounter daily limitations and struggles that, while not necessarily rising to the level of sin, still are present opportunities for us to become angry or disappointed in ourselves: times when we accidentally promise more than we can deliver, disappoint the people we love, or struggle to handle the pressures of life as well as we might like. In these times our natural response is often to fall prey to the angry inner critic that lives in our heads. We'll talk about how to address these negative messages in a moment, but there is an important step to take before entering into any internal battle against the lies Satan would have us believe about ourselves. We must run to God like a boxer going to his corner to receive counsel from his coach before the fight. Before the voices in your head start yelling at you, before you give into those feelings of shame and anger when confronted by your weakness and imperfections, run—don't walk—to God.

> Heavenly Father, I am mourning my imperfections, my limitations, and my weakness. I feel obliged to condemn myself for all the ways I don't feel like enough for my job, my wife, my family, for you. Help me. Let me lean on you. Hold me up, because I know that I am not strong enough. Not only that, but the people I care about know it too, and I feel ashamed. I am mourning all that I am not. Your Son promised that all those who mourn will be consoled. I am asking for your consolation. Help me to love myself despite my weaknesses and imperfections.

> Teach me to be compassionate toward myself as you are compassionate with me. And help me share that compassion with those who are hurting and who are leaning on me. I ask this through Jesus Christ my Lord and the intercession of St. Joseph. Amen.

## Questions for Reflection

- When do you tend to feel angry or disappointed with yourself? How do you usually respond?
- What would change if you could, in these times, allow yourself to experience God's compassion and mercy?

### *2. Master your inner voice.*

St. Ignatius of Loyola referred to any thought, feeling, or impulse that pulled us away from God or made it harder to be the people God was calling us to be a "desolation." A desolation is the movement of an evil spirit whispering in our spiritual ears, asking us to dwell on the worst of ourselves instead of reflecting on the grace and mercy of God. Desolations stand in contrast to "consolations," which represent the whisperings of the Holy Spirit, drawing us closer to God or gently encouraging us to cooperate with God's grace more effectively. When we are being influenced by consolations, we tend to experience meaningfulness, intimacy, and virtue. That is, we tend to, respectively, be aware of our how we can use our gifts to respond to the challenges before us, draw closer to others, and take advantage of any support or comfort our relationships offer and remain open to the growth opportunities life affords us in good times and bad. By contrast, when we are under the influence of desolations, we tend to experience a sense of powerlessness ("there's nothing I can do"), isolation ("no one cares/I shouldn't burden them"), and self-pity or self-indulgence ("there's nothing to do except make myself feel better in whatever way I can"). We will not find these qualities listed among the gifts and fruits of the Holy Spirit. Any time we become aware of thoughts or feelings that we could characterize as desolations, we must come against these thoughts. I describe a process for doing this in my books, *Broken Gods: Hope, Healing, and the Seven Longings of the Human Heart* and *God Help Me! This Stress Is Driving Me Crazy: Finding Balance through God's Grace*. For a more developed understanding of how to win the battle against desolations, I encourage you to refer to those titles. The short version is that we need to fight against these desolations by

1. recognizing that they are not sources of counsel, wisdom, strength, or change but rather temptations from Satan to wallow and make things worse;
2. actively recalling times when we did respond well to challenges, did enjoy the support of others, were open to learning and growing, and did feel the presence and power of God;
3. imagining how we would respond to the present struggles if we could feel the things we identified in step 2. These represent our true or authentic selves;
4. acting "as if" we feel the things we identified in step 2 and 3 even if we don't feel those thing currently. If we act as if we are in touch with our true selves (that is, who we are when we are in touch with God's grace and the consolations of the Holy Spirit) then the truth will set us free from our present struggles.

## Questions for Reflection

- To what common desolations do you fall prey?
- How might you respond differently to them in the future, knowing what you know now?

### *3. Dwell on his mercy.*

There will be times that these desolations are very strong and continue to affect us even though we are fighting against them. In these times, we must again recall our Lord's words to St. Paul: "My grace is sufficient for you" (2 Cor 12:9). Instead of dwelling on your lack, rest in God's compassion. God mourns with us when we bring him the frustrations we feel with ourselves, and the compassion we encounter in his presence transforms us into something greater than we could ever imagine. Remember the words of St. John Paul II, who said, "We are not the sum of our weaknesses and failures; we are the sum of the Father's love for us and our real capacity to become the image of his Son."

It might be true that for now, at least, certain battles cannot be ours to win, but God still has the victory, and we will be victorious through him if we remember that we are not defined by our successes or failures but by God's work in us and through us. It is critical that we regularly call to mind—and keep track of—those times when we feel particularly connected to God's mercy and love. Simple practices—like keeping a prayer journal in which you record moments of grace for future reference or observing certain sacramentals like a favorite medal or holy card—can serve as anchors, bringing us back to those sacred moments when your connection to God's presence was real and clear. Take advantage of these reminders in those times when you are feeling weak, imperfect, or all too aware of your limitations. Call to mind that God loves you not for what you can accomplish for him but for who you are to him: his beloved son in whom he is well pleased (see Mk 1:11).

## Questions for Reflection

- When are you most in touch with God's mercy and love? What things do you do to hold on to these moments of grace?
- What difference would it make in your life if you could hold onto these moments in times when you are prone to beat up on yourself?

### *4. Accept responsibility.*

Consolations, by contrast, lead to a new, healthy, and freeing sense of responsibility. We often think of the word *responsibility* as an oppressive term. Most of us don't experience this word as freeing, but if we can break out of places of desolation then responsibility is a terrifically freeing word.

When we are consumed by desolations, we view the word *responsibility* as a synonym for "blame," "fault," or "obligation." But in the spirit of consolation, we can experience responsibility in its best sense: namely, having the free and conscious *ability to respond* in grace-filled ways to the challenges we face.

Getting past desolations and reconnecting with God's mercy and love in times when we are tempted to be self-condemning isn't just about making ourselves feel better. It is also about becoming more effective tools in God's hands. Having forgiven ourselves and allowed ourselves to be robed in God's mercy, we can spare the emotional and spiritual energy to be merciful to others. Having learned to encounter God's love in our weakness, we can deal more lovingly with the weaknesses we encounter in our wives, our children, and others. Instead of living in constant states of reaction because our emotional and spiritual resources are consumed by self-pity and self-loathing, we can become genuine conduits of grace and healing in our families. We can be the lights that lead our spouses, our children, and everyone we encounter into a deeper relationship with God.

In the end, accepting responsibility means asking ourselves the question, "What is one small thing I can do, in this moment, to nudge things along from the way they are to the way they need to be so that God's glory can shine out here in this place, at this time, through this person?" When I can adopt this attitude I can both empathize with my spouse and children and support them in the changes God may be asking of them. I don't have to save everyone. I don't have to make everything work on my own power. I just have to be present and then freely and consciously choose to do one small thing to respond to the challenge in front of me. In doing so, I can stop being a stumbling block to myself, my wife, and my children and, instead, begin to experience the gentle but formidable power of my role as a Christian father. I can become an agent of loving, merciful, graceful change in my home.

### Questions for Reflection

- When have you felt God using you to make a difference in the life of another person?
- Instead of responding with blame or defensiveness, how can you do more to respond in loving and merciful ways to the shortcomings you see in others?

### Prayer

Heavenly Father, give me the grace to listen only to you. I give you my inner dialog and ask you to sanctify the words I say to myself about you, myself, and the world around me. Let my thoughts glorify you and enable me to know your will and follow your plan for my life in everything I do. Amen.

## *Blessed Are the Dads Who Mourn*

### Your Relationship with Your Wife

Holding onto this ability to respond is key to practicing the second Beatitude with your wife because it allows you to be emotionally present in your marriage. It is a blessing to be able to mourn with your wife, to have compassion for her struggles, and to stand with her in times of difficulty. So often I hear from women who cannot count on their husbands to be there when they are struggling or sad. Too many men feel put on the spot by their wives' emotions. Some pop-psych authors suggest this is because men feel pressured to "fix" their wives' feelings. Maybe. Maybe not. But this doesn't account for all the men who are unwilling to hear their wives' feelings in the first place. After all, you can't fix what you aren't willing to recognize. I think the problem runs deeper.

In my experience working with couples, the reason men are unwilling to be emotionally present to their wives is that they assume that if their wives are unhappy it is a judgment on them. Too many men, seeing their wives sad, angry, or frustrated, think it means, "You're screwing up. You have failed." This is especially true when our wives are frustrated with us for some reason.

Jesus says, "Blessed are they who mourn, for they will be comforted" (Mt 5:4). Practicing this BeDADitude in marriage means allowing your wife to feel what she feels without taking it personally. Even when she's upset with you, it may not have anything to do with you (for instance, she may be tired or already irritated with the kids), and even when she is righteously angry or upset because of something you did, that is merely a problem to be addressed together, not an indictment of your failure as a man. To practice this second BeDADitude in your marriage, consider the following:

1. Don't personalize.
2. Empathize.
3. Be responsible.

### *1. Don't personalize.*

Remember, even when she is upset with you, you are not the problem. The problem is the problem. You and she must work together to solve the problem. You can't do that if you take everything she says personally. "Well," you might say, "if she's complaining about me, how am I not supposed to take that personally?"

The answer, of course, is to realize that she is not complaining about you as much as she may be complaining about something you did or did not do. You are not the things you do or don't do. Remember the quote from St. John Paul II mentioned earlier: "We are not the sum of our weaknesses and failures; we are the sum of the Father's love for us and our real capacity to become the image of his Son."

Whether your wife is upset with you or just upset, she doesn't need or want you to make it about you. She needs to know that you understand her pain and that you care about helping her find a way out of it. Step one in this process is standing up to the temptation welling up inside of you to make this all about you. Take a breath. Remember that God loves you and is asking you to share this love with her.

### *2. Empathize.*

Believe it or not, empathy is a natural skill for women and men. It is a natural function of the social brain. Unfortunately, many men are parented in a way that damages their social brains growing up. We are raised in a fashion that robs us of our God-given, natural capacities for empathy. God wants to give that ability back to you. In fact, he needs you to learn it. St. John Paul II's theology of the body reminds us that all human beings—women and men—were created for communion and are destined to spend eternity in the intimate communion with God and others that is heaven. Without empathy, however, there is no communion. Empathy is the function of the social brain that allows your so-called "mirror neurons" to recreate a little bit of what another person is feeling inside of yourself so you can identify with it and respond accordingly. If you watch me bump my head, chances are you'll wince, because your mirror neurons light up and remind you of what it feels like to be hurt in a similar way. This, in turn, allows you to ask if I'm OK and to offer to help me out. When empathy is impaired, people cannot feel what others are feeling. Instead, they respond to the pain of others with confusion, anger, or even sadistic laughter.

Men are often parented in an arm's-length, affectionless manner that leads to the underdevelopment of their social brains and robs them of their full capacity for empathy. This lack is not a natural male trait, nor is it admirable. It is an antisocial trait that negatively impacts moral reasoning and Christian compassion. You can't be moved to fix what you won't allow yourself to feel. When men are raised properly, although they may express it differently, their brains can develop as much a capacity for empathy as women have. After all, Jesus represents the fullness of masculinity, and it is hard to imagine a man who exhibited more empathy and compassion than our Lord.

So how do you develop your God-given capacity for empathy, especially for your wife? Simple. Care about her and share with her. Caring about her means really listening and asking questions that enable you to understand her experience from the inside out. Care is a necessary aspect of respect. If you respect someone, you don't just avoid being mean to this person. You actively try to see the world through this person's eyes. You don't have to agree with him. You just have to care enough about him to want to understand why he feels as he does. Asking questions like, "What does it mean to you that thus and such happened?"; "How did it make you feel when so and so said that?"; and "What was it like for you when that happened?", helps you get inside your wife's experience so that, whether you agree with her or not, you can activate your mirror neurons and share in her feelings in the moment.

In addition to caring, sharing is an important part of empathy. Empathy says, "I know how you feel." How do you communicate that you "get" how someone else feels? You relate times when you think you felt similarly to your wife. For instance, "You know, telling me about how your mom made you feel on the phone today reminds me of that time when my dad said he was disappointed in me. I was crushed. Is that how you feel?"

When sharing some of your experiences, be careful not to steal the conversation and make it all about you. Don't ever say, "I know *just* how you feel. It's *just* like . . ." You never really know exactly how someone else feels. You just want to let them know that you are in the same ballpark—emotionally speaking. Care enough to listen. Share enough to let her know you heard.

### *3. Be responsible.*

Being responsible in the face of your wife's feelings does not necessarily mean accepting blame or agreeing with her conclusions or even fixing things for her—although there may be times when any and all of these options could be appropriate. It just means that you have the ability to respond in some way to her feelings that makes her feel genuinely cared for and affirmed by your presence. If you don't know how to respond, just ask, "Honey, I'm so sorry you're going through this. I love you. What can I do to help?"

Often, she'll tell you. If she does, go do that thing. Don't argue with her or tell her that what she asked for is silly. Just do it. Of course, just as often she might say, "I don't know," or, "Nothing." That just means she needs some time. Hold her. Tell her again that you love her. Tell her you're sorry she's hurting. Later, do something she isn't expecting that you know will make her feel cherished. Don't tease her or make a pass at her unless you are 100 percent sure that she wants you to. Instead, do something that you know makes her life easier or more pleasant. Do a job she hates to do around the house. Get her a card. Have some flowers delivered. Write her a note that says why you believe in her even when she's having a hard time believing in herself. Give her genuine compliments. You don't have to make a big production of it. In fact, it's much better if you don't. Just do little things that say, "When you are feeling low, you can count on me to make your life better." Your willingness to mourn with your wife when she is sad or frustrated and to empathize with her concerns will lead to abundant blessings in your marriage.

### Questions for Reflection

- When do you feel most intimidated by your wife's emotions?
- What things can you do next time that will enable you to do a better job empathizing and letting her know she can count on you when she's feeling low?

### Prayer

Heavenly Father, give me the courage to mourn with my wife. Help me to not be afraid of her feelings, to not take her disappointments and frustrations as failures on my part but as opportunities to love her and serve her just as you would. Let me be your peace, consolation, and loving counsel to my bride, and let her rejoice in the emotional comfort and closeness you are able to provide to her through me. Amen.

## *Blessed Are the Dads Who Mourn*

### Your Relationship with Your Children

Everything I wrote about applying the second Beatitude to your relationship with your wife applies to your children as well. Your children need to know that their father loves them. Not "in his own way," as the lame excuse goes, but up close and personal in a way that their own experience of you cannot deny. When your children think of you, the first word that ought to come to mind is "support."

We all want to be strong fathers. We want our children to look up to us. To admire us, to see us as examples. To turn to us for life's important lessons. This is a good and godly desire. God created this desire within us and, moreover, created a way that this desire would be fulfilled. It's called attachment. God has created structures in your children's social brains that make them open up when they feel understood by someone. Feeling understood and empathized with stimulates the social brain's attachment centers, which facilitate a sense of bonding and connection. The thing is, we listen to whomever we feel attached. The more our kids feel like we share their feelings and "get" their struggles—mourn with them, as the Beatitude puts it—the more likely they will listen to us and allow us to disciple them. We cannot scare, threaten, or punish our children into discipleship relationships with us ("Fathers, do not provoke your children, so they may not become discouraged" [Col 3:21; see Eph 6:4]). We can only invite them to listen and learn from us by first showing them that they are worth our time and that we are willing to listen with hearts of empathy.

God wants our children to experience him through our examples. Studies in the psychology of faith development consistently show that your children's image of their heavenly Father begins with them projecting their vision of you onto God. Whether they can transition easily into authentic relationships with the real face of God or if they have to do a lot of work relearning who God truly is in adulthood has a lot to do with what kind of father you are to them today. What do we know about the character of God the Father?

> Before they call, I will answer; while they are yet speaking, I will hear. (Is 65:24)
>
> Come to me . . . and I will give you rest. (Mt 11:28)
>
> The Lord, the Lord, a God gracious and merciful, slow to anger and abounding in love and fidelity. (Ex 34:6)
>
> But you, Lord, are a compassionate and gracious God, slow to anger, abounding in mercy and truth. (Ps 86:15)

> As a father has compassion on his children, so the LORD has compassion on those who fear him. (Ps 103:13)

> Sing out, heavens, and rejoice, earth, break forth into song, you mountains, for the LORD comforts his people and shows mercy to his afflicted. (Is 49:13)

> If you then, who are wicked, know how to give good gifts to your children, how much more will your heavenly Father give good things to those who ask him? (Mt 7:11)

God is a compassionate, loving, empathetic Father who feels his children's pain, mourns with them, hears their cries, and responds promptly, generously, and consistently to their concerns. In fact, God the Father's love for his children is so powerful and tangible it rivals or even exceeds the love of a nursing mother.

> Can a mother forget her infant, be without tenderness for the child of her womb? Even should she forget, I will never forget you. See, upon the palms of my hands I have engraved you; your walls are ever before me. (Is 49:15–16)

We as godly fathers cannot be embarrassed to shower affection and attention on our children. We must take after our heavenly Father in our slowness to anger, our great love and kindness, and our willingness to mourn with our children. Comforting children is not just a mother's job. A mother's consolation conveys warmth and acceptance, but a father's consolation conveys strength as well. When our children are crying or sad and we give them our time, lend our ear, hold them in our arms, and show them that we understand them, they feel empowered to go out and take on the world. Just like our heavenly Father's compassion gives his children the strength they need to go out and build the kingdom of God, a father's compassion emboldens his children to overcome the challenges that stand in the way of their becoming everything God created them to be. When your children come to you with their concerns, work hard not to take their feelings personally but to empathize with their experiences. Using similar steps as the ones I described in our discussion on empathizing with your wife, look for little ways to cherish your kids, build them up, and make their lives a little easier or more pleasant. No, you probably won't send your twelve-year-old son flowers. But you might do one of his chores when he's had a tough day, take him out for ice cream, or play his favorite game even if you're tired. Your presence and approval means everything to your kids. Go out of your way to share your feelings for and with your kids, and you will be blessed indeed.

## Questions for Reflection

- When do you find it hard to empathize with your kids?
- The next time your children need you, how will you do a better job not taking their feelings and actions personally and instead empathizing with their concerns and working to make their lives a little easier or more pleasant?

The second Beatitude gives God's sons the opportunity to forgive themselves and then practice that loving mercy with their spouses and children. When you struggle to be emotionally present and to empathize with your own struggles or the struggles of your wife and children, keep the following prayer in mind and know that God is with you.

## Prayer

Heavenly Father, you show me your compassion a million times a day. When I am sad and struggling, you mourn with me, and through your loving presence you transform me into the image of your Son. When my wife and children are sad or struggling, give me the courage to mourn with them. Help me not to see their sadness or frustration as personal condemnations but as expressions of pain requiring a compassionate response. Fill my heart with your love so that the compassion I share with my hurting family transforms them in the light of your grace and draws us to new life in you. Amen.

# THE THIRD BeDADitude

## Blessed are the dads who are meek. They will inherit the land.

When I speak at men's conferences, many husbands and fathers come to my table and ask, "I know I'm supposed to lead my family, but how do I know what the right way to lead them is?"

The surprising answer, of course, is to ask them and listen to what they say! Ask your wife and children what they need to be happy and fulfilled, and then help them find godly ways to do whatever they tell you.

A willingness to listen is the essence of meekness, and meekness is the engine that drives servant leadership. We men are often convinced that we have to be know-it-all psychics who are able to discern from various mysterious signs and portents what our families need and how we are best able to serve them. In the third BeDADitude, Jesus reminds us, again, that it is not up to us. We do not lead and serve by our own power. We lead and serve by listening.

Meekness is a tough quality for many men to relate to because it implies the exact opposite of what we think men are supposed to be. Meekness is not weakness. Nor is it cowardice, shyness, or passivity. Meekness represents a willingness to listen to and to learn from the experiences of others. It is the opposite of pride, which has Satan saying "I will *not* serve." In Matthew 11:29 Jesus uses the word *meek* to refer to a willingness to take up the yoke he would place upon his followers; that is to say, Jesus uses this word to describe a willingness to learn and follow our Lord's example of faithful service.

The father who is meek is not absent, emotionally withdrawn, or hangdog. He is actively engaged in learning what his family needs and finding godly ways to help them meet those needs.

## Blessed Are the Dads Who Are Meek

### Your Relationship with God

The meek father and husband is first and foremost a man who listens. The truly meek man is not bumbling, incompetent, or socially awkward—all things people often associate with meekness. Rather, the man who is meek merely has a receptive heart. He knows that to lead and serve he must first ask what the people in his care need from him. He begins to train his heart to be open to listening to others by training himself to listen to God so that he might know how best to serve God with his whole heart, mind, and strength.

In the chapter on the first BeDADitude—"Blessed are the dads who are poor in spirit"—our discussion on prayer mainly focused on talking to God, but that is only half of it. Prayer is supposed to be a conversation with God. One where he actually talks back. This idea is actually fairly intimidating to many Catholics. A prominent Catholic publisher I know once commented to me, "I always hear people saying that God talked to them. 'God told me this.' 'God said that.' What does that even mean? I don't think I've ever heard him talking to me."

Here was a man who dedicated his entire life to serving God's kingdom and spreading the Word. He could have been successful in any business, and yet, for some mysterious reason, he chose Catholic publishing. Obviously God was talking to him, and he was even listening to one degree or another, but he couldn't bring himself to recognize it or even participate in the conversation in any intentional way because it seemed too strange. And how sadly common this view is!

The truth is, God does want to talk to us, but we need to know how to listen. It is beyond the scope of this book to give you all the ways you can hear God talking back to you, but we can cover some of the basics. St. Ignatius of Loyola, a soldier-saint and the founder of the Jesuit order, spoke of three ways God speaks to us: total clarity, an attraction of the heart, and the weight of reason.

These three means by which God speaks to us assume a few things. First, they assume that we are seeking to live holy lives. We can't expect to hear God if we aren't actively trying to learn his ways, and he will never ask us to do something that goes against the Ten Commandments or Church teaching—because doing that would contradict the conversation God has been having with humankind for thousands of years.

Second, they assume we are in a state of grace. Sin darkens the intellect (see Eph 4:18). It separates us from God. Trying to hear him when we are in a state of sin is like trying to hear a friend talking across a busy street. You know he's saying something but . . . what was that? I'm reminded of the scene from Monty Python's *Life of Brian* where a crowd of Jewish peasants can't hear Jesus' words, and they say, "Blessed are the . . . cheesemakers? What's so special about the cheesemakers?" Regular Confession and a contrite heart open up the channels of grace that unstop our ears and help us hear God.

Finally, they assume that we will always test what we think God is saying to us. First, we test what we think by applying the consolation/desolation test we discussed earlier. Does the message you're receiving nudge you toward meaningfulness, intimacy, and virtue, or does it push you toward powerlessness, isolation, and self-pity/self-indulgence? The former is from God. The latter? Not so much. The second way we test what we think God is saying to us is by getting regular spiritual direction or at least having regular conversations with someone whom we consider to be more spiritually mature than ourselves. Hearing God's voice correctly can be tricky. It's helpful to check what we think we're hearing with someone who is a little further down the road, spiritually speaking. And with that preamble, let's look at the three primary ways God talks back to us:

1. Total clarity.
2. An attraction of the heart.
3. The weight of reason.

### *1. Total clarity.*

This is the most wonderful and rarest way God talks to us. This happened to me when I proposed to my wife. I was planning to propose in several months, but we had just finished praying together, and I felt this incredible sense of rightness. I knew beyond a shadow of a doubt—with 100 percent certainty—that I needed to ask her to marry me right then. It was what God wanted. I was sure of it. This wasn't some impulse from me. I knew that. This wasn't my plan at all. I knew exactly how I wanted to ask her to marry me. This wasn't it. But it didn't matter. I knew what God wanted. He moved every part of me in that moment in a very particular direction, and there was nothing else I could do except get out of his way and let it happen. Of course, I could have refused, but no part of me wanted to. Everything came together and made sense. Thirty years later, it is still making sense.

As I said, this is the rarest way God speaks to us. It usually happens around major events, and when it happens, you can't deny it. It is absolute. You can't do anything to make this happen. One minute you are minding your own business; the next minute everything about you is fascinated and focused on this one thing, and it all just makes sense: of course you are going to do this. Yes, you could resist it. God never removes our free will, but in these rare moments of total clarity, it just seems ridiculous to resist it.

Sometimes, we will even hear God speaking—in a sense—in our hearts. I have also had this happen. When I am praying, I will sometimes hear a voice speak in my heart. It is like self-talk, but it isn't my voice, and it is accompanied by a sense of total peace and understanding that I couldn't create for myself no matter how hard I tried. This is rarer still, but it happens.

For example, after my wife and I were married, in prayer I once "heard" God's voice speaking in my heart that within two years she would be healed of a serious illness she was struggling with. I didn't know what to make of it. I praised him for it, and I shared it with my wife in a "hey, I just wanted to encourage you" kind of way, but since I couldn't do anything about it, I tried not to put too much stock in it. Regardless, two years later, almost to the day, she was indeed completely recovered. Considering the nature of the illness, her recovery was miraculous, but I wasn't at all surprised because, even though I actively tried to deny it so as not to get my hopes up, all the while I kept hearing that she would be healed within two years and that God was giving us this gift that we might know that he was the Lord of our lives. Either way, when God uses this means of communication, you can't deny it even when you try to. It simply is.

### *2. An attraction of the heart.*

Sometimes, God communicates to us in a manner that reflects the breaking of the dawn. At first, when we bring particular questions to him, there is nothing but darkness, but as we sit with the questions, continue to pray, reflect on how the events of our days/weeks/months inform our decision, and seek consultation, we slowly come to a place where we "just know" the right thing to do. This process requires diligence and effort, but it goes beyond mere reason. This is different from those times where we gather more information and a winner clearly emerges. It is more intuitive, more of a "sense" that something is clearly the right choice even though we are at a loss to explain exactly why. It just feels like the right choice, and it feels "right-er" the more we pray and reflect upon it. Often, God speaks to us this way when we have to choose between two good things, either of which could be perfectly fine options. As with total clarity, we often have a very clear sense that these feelings of rightness are growing within us but do not come from us.

### *3. The weight of reason.*

The third way St. Ignatius suggests God speaks to us is the most common and the most misunderstood. In this mode of communication, as we pray, reflect, and seek consultation about a decision, we gather more information and see clearly—by the weight of the evidence and the power of reason—that one choice is superior to others. Most of the time, we simply think that we have made decisions, but this attitude gives God short shrift. We have no power on our own. We broken, sinful people certainly have no power to choose what is true, good, and right on our own power. I know from an honest appraisal of my own struggles that if I manage to make a good choice about anything, I must have had a lot of help!

Even when people understand that prayer and grace play a role in the normal process of good decision-making, they sometimes struggle to act on the weight of reason because they trip over the question, "How do I know if this is God's will versus my will?" Although the person asking this question has his heart in the right place, this represents a bit of magical thinking. We tend to discount the natural ways God speaks to us. We assume that if God is speaking, it has to be a Michael Bay production with a huge pyrotechnics budget. We forget the lesson Elijah learned when he was waiting for an answer from God on Mt. Horeb. When God finally responded to his prayer, his voice was not in the hurricane or the earthquake or the great fire that Elijah witnessed (talk about a bad camping trip) but in the gentle breeze that followed all these (literally) earth-shattering events (see 1 Kgs 19:11–13).

The truth is, anytime we choose something that leads us toward greater experiences of meaningfulness, intimacy, or virtue (over powerlessness, isolation, and self-pity/self-indulgence) in our lives, it is because we are hearing—on some level—the consolations of the Holy Spirit leading us and guiding us. God gave us our will and our reason so that he could speak to us through them. As long as we consistently join our will and reason to prayer, repentance, reflection, and consultation, God will communicate to us constantly. We don't have to worry whether it is our desire or his. If the voice (either in our own heads or coming from someone else's mouth) we are hearing leads us to greater meaningfulness, intimacy, and virtue, it is always God's voice speaking to us. We do well when we listen.

The meek man is the man who longs to hear God's voice and seeks to quiet the conflicting passions and voices in his own head so that he can clearly hear God when he speaks. Again, meekness is not weakness. Properly understood, meekness is a stillness of the spirit, a calm that says, "Speak Lord, I am listening. Not my will, but yours."

The man who is meek is empowered to inherit the earth because he has learned to quiet himself enough to hear God teaching him how to become the master of creation that he was created to be (see Gn 2:15).

## Questions for Reflection

- When has God made himself known to you with total clarity? Have you ever heard him or experienced him moving your attention and will in a manner that was beyond all doubt? When was this, and what did God ask you to do?

- When have you heard God speak to you as an attraction of the heart? Did you recognize it as his voice? Is he currently speaking to you in this way about a decision in your life?
- What difference would it make to think that God was speaking to you through your will and reason? How would it change your perception of God's involvement in your life if you could acknowledge his voice behind every choice you made that led to greater meaningfulness, intimacy, and virtue in your life?

### Prayer

Heavenly Father, teach me to have the meekness that allows me to hear your voice, to truly listen to your small, still voice speaking in my heart, informing my mind, forming my will. Help me know how to attend to your voice, that I might inherit the earth and learn to care for all that you have given to me in a manner that reflects your face to the world. Amen.

## *Blessed Are the Dads Who Are Meek*

### Your Relationship with Your Wife

Ephesians 5:23 tells us, "The husband is the head of his wife just as Christ is the head of the church." Our headship is not absolute, however. It is dependent upon our willingness to serve a particular mission, namely, to love our wives: "Husbands, love your wives, even as Christ loved the church and handed himself over for her to sanctify her, cleansing her by the bath of water with the word, that he might present to himself the church in splendor, without spot or wrinkle or any such thing, that she might be holy and without blemish" (Eph 5:25–27). We are to love our wives "as [our] own bodies" (Eph 5:28).

This relationship has been described by many as one of servant leadership, but getting servant leadership right requires a spirit of meekness. Too often, in the attempt to be servant leaders in their households, men behave more like parents to their wives instead of partners.

Too often, in a genuine attempt to be leaders, men think that it is their job to set the agenda. It is their job to tell everyone—including their wives—what they have a right to need or want. The man who does this exceeds his authority. God has planted in each of his children certain needs that must be met for that person to develop into a fully formed son or daughter of God. We do not get to deny what God has planted. If we do so, we sow resentment and discord in our homes. We do violence against God and our spouses. It is not our place—ever—to tell our wives what she has a right to need. It is only our place to help her get her needs met in a manner that is godly and respectful of the needs of the others in the family. That is the role of a partner and helpmate.

The meek man understands this. The meek husband is not a milquetoast who allows his wife to do whatever she wants, however she wants, whenever she wants. I know it is meant as a joke, but in my opinion, there is a special place in hell for the man who truly believes the popular saying that the secret to a happy marriage is learning to say, "Yes, dear." Such a man will become a nonperson in his marriage and will breed resentment in his wife for his lack of genuine interest or involvement in his marriage and family life.

On the other hand, the meek man is not a tyrant. Nor is he a parent who tells his wife what she has a right to need or want. Rather, the meek man seeks to cultivate a listening heart. He asks his wife what she needs and wants, prays with her, works with her, and discusses with her the best ways and means to achieve those things. As they talk and pray about what she wants, they consider—together—what God is asking of them and what the needs of the others in the house are. The husband facilitates the process by which God's will and the common good are served in the home. The servant leader who has mastered the art of meekness asserts himself as the master of the process of decision-making, not the adjudicator of the outcome of decision-making. This latter work is seen as God's job, for the meek man recognizes that God is the true head of household.

The meek servant leader inherits the love and devotion of his wife because she comes to see him as a man who is willing to listen to her deepest needs and help her find ways to meet those needs in a manner that is godly and ecological—that is, respectful of the common good of the house. He never lets her give up on her needs just because it is hard to figure out how to meet them, but he never lets her just impulsively act without considering God's will and the common good. And he obeys these same principles in seeking his own needs and wants. In a sense, the godly husband as meek servant leader never negotiates what his wife says she needs, but he insists that the how and when (that is, the process by which these needs are met) be subject to God's will and the common good of the household. It often takes time and creativity to make this happen, but the godly and meek servant leader, having listened to and heard what God has written on his wife's heart, is a fierce champion of his wife's needs, even when it takes time and effort to figure out how to meet them. As a result, he inherits her love and devotion, and she trusts him with the deepest parts of her heart.

### *Needs versus wants.*

This is usually the point where someone says, "Well sure, we all have a right to get our needs met. But surely we don't have a right to get everything we want." There is some truth in this statement, but it's easily abused in marriage. Too often, husbands arbitrarily classify genuine needs their wives may have as wants simply because they are inconvenient, difficult to meet, or demanding in ways that are moral and reasonable but uncomfortable. The husband that gives into this temptation claims more authority than God has given him.

So what is the right way to distinguish needs from wants? Think of a "need" as anything that sustains my overall well-being and fosters the full development of my physical, psychological, spiritual, or relational health. Because needs must be met in order for people to become the fully developed persons God created them to be, Christians have a God-given right to have all of their needs met.

A "want," by contrast, is not a "lesser need" or an optional or inconvenient need. It is simply the means by which I prefer to meet a need. The need represents what is missing and must be fulfilled so that I can be a healthy, happy, well-developed person. The want is the means by which (and timeframe in which) I prefer to acquire the thing that is missing. The only way to respectfully deal with wants is to listen for the need that someone is attempting to serve and then present a healthier, godlier alternative to meet that need.

Here is a simple way to practice this. If your wife ever asks you for something that seems crazy, useless, pointless, or frustrating, check yourself. Don't try to talk her out of it. Instead, ask her the following question: "If you got that, help me understand what it would do for you. How do you imagine that doing that/ getting that would make your life better?" Sometimes it takes a few go-rounds to get the answer, but once you have the answer, you have identified the need behind the (seemingly) absurd or unworkable want. Having figured out the need, it is now your job to pray with your wife and discuss and brainstorm creative, godly, healthier ways to meet that need that will honor God's will and respect the common good of the house.

If you have historically been the sort of husband who has told your wife what she should or shouldn't want—or if your wife was raised in a controlling household—you might get some pushback when you attempt to find healthier ways to get her needs met. Having never encountered someone who was really committed to helping her meet her needs, she might be afraid to submit her wants to this process. Just keep reassuring her that if you can't help her figure out a genuinely better way to help her get her need met, you will also defer to her want, but insist that she work with you through the process of praying, discussing, and brainstorming alternatives first. In time, she will come to see that you aren't trying to play tricks on her or manipulate her but are genuinely committed to listening to her, learning her needs, and being the sort of meek servant leader that helps her get everything she needs out of life in a manner that is both godly and respectful of the common good of the household. She will also see that you are willing to do this even when it causes you to stretch and grow and become more of the meaningful, intimate, and virtuous husband you are meant to be. This is the way that you will invite your wife to submit to you, and in your meekness and your willingness to listen, learn, and lead, you will inherit her love and devotion in the process.

## Questions for Reflection

- How does this approach to servant leadership differ from your previous thoughts about the same?
- How would practicing meekness—in the sense of cultivating a listening heart for your wife's needs and wants—change your relationship with your wife? What needs and wants must you be more sensitive to in the future?

## Prayer

Heavenly Father, help me to cultivate a meek, listening heart for my wife. Help me to check my pride and my love of comfort and instead meet her needs and wants as her champion. Give me the wisdom, creativity, and dedication I need to show my wife that her needs—even the ones I don't fully understand or appreciate—are important to me and that I am committed to helping her find godly ways to get everything she needs to become the fully formed, healthy, holy, and happy woman you created her to be. Amen.

## *Blessed Are the Dads Who Are Meek*

### Your Relationship with Your Children

Listening to God and our wives gives us good practice for cultivating meek, listening hearts with our children as well. All fathers want children who will obey them, learn from them, and see them as role models. In the last chapter on mourning, we discussed the power of empathy for turning your children's hearts toward you. Now we'll explore how meekness is the key to inheriting your children's obedience.

Fathers tend to fall into one of two parenting traps. Some are authoritarian. They insist on blind obedience from their children and enforce rules with heavy-handed approaches to discipline. Others are largely permissive. They try to become their children's best friends, even when it means undermining their mother's attempts to raise godly young men and women.

Meekness is the antidote to both of these errors. Meekness allows fathers to be authoritative listeners of their children. It enables them to take the time to get to know their children's needs and then preside over the process whereby they teach their children godly ways to meet those needs in a manner that respects the common good.

In our discussion about meekness in your relationship with your wife, I outlined an approach to negotiation that allows you to listen to the need behind your wife's wants and partner with her to find alternative ways to help her meet those needs. Although, as I mentioned in that discussion, parents have an obligation to be more directive with their children than partners may be with each other, you can use a similar approach to teaching your children how to meet their needs and wants in good and godly ways.

It is absolutely true that sometimes a father simply must say no to his children. When children ask for things that would be objectively dangerous or bad for them, loving fathers must respond with an unequivocal, "I'm sorry, but no." Even so, these times are fairly rare.

For all but the most obviously, objectively problematic requests, the father who has mastered the art of meekness will take it upon himself to try to suggest alternative ways children may meet their needs or wants. For instance, it might not be appropriate for your child to have sweets before dinner, but rather than offering a blanket "no," you might say, "You can't have a cookie now, but if you would still like one after you have eaten a healthy dinner, you may have a cookie then."

The same applies to more complicated situations. "I would love for you to be able to get your license, but I need to see you being more responsible around the house before I can trust you behind the wheel. For the next month, I want to see you doing your chores without being asked and controlling your temper when your brother irritates you. If I can see you paying attention and controlling your reactions at home, I will have a better sense that you can do those things behind the wheel and avoid an accident. We'll talk about your progress every week and reevaluate where things stand at the end of the month."

When we adopt this strategy—instead of just reacting with a lazy no every time our children ask for something that makes us the slightest bit uncomfortable—we send an important message to our kids: namely, "I am the person you can come to with whatever needs and wants you have, and I will teach you godly ways to either meet or manage your desires." The father who is meek enough to listen to his children instead of shutting them down inherits their respect, devotion, and obedience. Because they know their father will listen until he understands what they truly want and will always be prepared to help them find godly ways to get what they want if at all possible, they go to him, ask his counsel, and listen to what he says. And when he does say no—because nine out of ten times he gives at least a qualified yes—they know he means it and that the matter is settled. Children don't wheedle and whine to get what they want from a father who has mastered the art of meekness, because they know he is on their side and that his yes is a considered yes and his no is a thoughtful no and that both answers are given with their best interests—not the parent's laziness or irritation—in mind.

Of course, this isn't meant to be a parenting book. For more ideas on how to be an effective disciplinarian, please check out *Parenting with Grace: The Catholic Parents' Guide to Raising Almost Perfect Kids*. The point here is that meekness is the key to cultivating discipleship hearts in your children. If you want your children to turn their hearts toward you, to bring their desires and needs to you rather than their friends or some other adult who could undermine you, then you must show them that you are willing to listen—really listen—and consider all their requests. You don't have to say yes to them, but you do have to listen well enough to understand why they imagine getting that thing or having that privilege would make their lives better. Then, more often than not, you can suggest godlier ways by which they could meet those needs or wants.

Raising your children to be your disciples means training up your children in the ways they should go so that in their old age they will not depart from it (see Prv 22:6). This does not just mean teaching them the rules and then enforcing the rules with heavy-handed consequences. It means training them how to manage all of their desires in godly ways and teaching them to meet their needs in a manner that reflects the common good of the family. This way, as they grow up and start to have their own families, they have a respectful model to use in bringing godly order to their own homes.

## Questions for Reflection

- Are there times when you find it difficult to truly listen to your children? How might you use the ideas from this chapter to be a more willing and receptive listener?
- Are there certain needs or wants your children express that you tend to deny without really understanding why they desire those things? How can you do a better job hearing the true needs behind their requests and giving them godly, respectful ways to meet those needs?

The third Beatitude tells us that the meek will inherit the earth. The father who embraces authentic meekness will become the king of his castle, winning the hearts of those in his care. He will be given the grace to exercise godly dominion over the people who love and depend upon him, leading his family to surrender their hearts to Christ one need, one desire at a time.

## Prayer

Heavenly Father, you generously hear all of our requests and supply all of our needs. Help us to respond to our children's needs with open hearts so that we might teach them to bring all of their needs and desires to you. Give us the patience and wisdom we need to enable our children to become everything you created them to be: godly, grace-filled young men and women who know how to meet their needs in a manner that gives glory to you and is respectful to those around them. Amen.

# The Fourth BeDADitude

## Blessed are the dads who hunger and thirst for righteousness. They will be satisfied.

What does it mean to hunger and thirst for righteousness? Does it mean that we must be so perpetually haunted by our need for grace that we forget to count on God's mercy? Should we be so consumed with our inadequacies and the imperfections of our wives and children that we suffocate ourselves and those around us with critical demands and disapproval, all so that we can motivate ourselves and those we love to be all they can be?

Certainly not. Remember God's admonition when St. Paul was attacking himself for his failures to live in complete righteousness on his own power: "My grace is sufficient" (2 Cor 12:9). So what can it mean, then?

The man who hungers and thirsts for righteousness knows who he is (a son of God) and is committed to spending his life becoming that. St. John Paul II once curiously said, "Become what you are." He meant that we are all mistaken when we look in the mirror and think we are seeing true reflections of ourselves. That merely reflects who we are now, but it does not reveal who God sees when he looks at us. That is who we truly are—saints!—and that is what we will spend our lives becoming.

We have a tendency to think of these saintly selves, these godly, grace-filled, whole and healed men, as if they were some other beings altogether, as if God intends us to spend each day killing ourselves to become something we aren't but somehow were meant to be. We need to reverse this. The fallen selves we see when we look in the (metaphorical) mirror aren't our true selves. Rather, we are what God sees in us. He has planted the seed of sanctity in us. The wheat is growing up among the weeds, and it is our job to cooperate with God's grace so that we can water and fertilize the wheat while allowing the chaff to slowly, patiently die off, revealing the abundant harvest God has planted within us (see Mt 13:24–30).

In the parable of the wheat and the weeds, the farmhands ask if they should go out and rip up the weeds planted by an enemy. The master counsels them to wait lest good wheat be pulled up with the tares. When we hate, attack, and berate ourselves (and those we love) for righteousness's sake, we are like the anxious farmhands, indiscriminately tearing up the good harvest with the bad. It would be better instead to recognize that God has planted much good in us and that, while the enemy has scattered bad seeds in the soil of our hearts as well, the best course of action is to starve the bad seeds while nourishing the good seeds with the light of God's love, the water of life, and the fertilizer that is our desire to cooperate with his grace. We will not be able to root out all the weeds on our own, but we can choke many of them off with the virtuous crop that God is growing in us, and in the end we can be confident in God's ability to separate out what is good and bad in us in the final harvest.

What does this mean in practice? It means having a clear sense of who we truly are and leaning in to these true selves as best as we can through mindful practice, prayer, repentance, and persistence. Throughout this chapter, we'll explore how to do this, first in our relationship with God, then with our wives, and finally with our children.

## *Blessed Are the Dads Who Hunger and Thirst for Righteousness*

### Your Relationship with God

Hungering for righteousness begins with a mission. We must know who we truly are and be able to identify the true selves we are becoming through God's grace. What is this mission? It consists of the qualities, the strengths, the virtues that we need in order to rise gracefully to the challenges we experience in our lives.

Would you ever send your child out to do something you knew he was doomed to fail at? Would you ever intentionally send your child out to look incompetent or foolish? Of course not. Again, if we who are evil want to spare our children from failure and humiliation, how much more does our heavenly Father want to save us from the same!

Unfortunately, we tend to doubt this on a regular basis. We often feel that we are in over our heads in some aspect of our lives. We assume that God has set us up or, at least, that he leaves a lot of room for our possible failure. Nonsense.

I don't mean to suggest that becoming our authentic, righteous selves is easy, nor do I mean that it is somehow impossible to fail. But just like when we send our children out into the world with the skills they need to do well in school or on the field, we are similarly equipped by our heavenly Father to succeed. If we can keep our wits about us and our eyes on him, we can be confident that he has given us everything we need to rise above the challenges we face—gracefully. How do we do this?

1. Identify the mission.
2. Get a coach.

### *1. Identify the mission.*

God can only begin to satisfy our hunger and thirst for righteousness when we can identify our mission—that is, when we have a clear sense of who we really are and where we are going. How do we accomplish this?

*Look to the end zone*: When you're on the field, you don't just run around randomly with the ball. You look for the end zone. You keep it in the forefront of your mind and run toward it with everything you have. The spiritual life is the same way. In any challenge you face, great or small, ask yourself, "What qualities or virtues would I need to respond to this challenge well—that is, in a manner that would give glory to God and enable me to be my best self?" Do you need patience? Courage? Fortitude? A sense of humor? Love? Identify the top two to three qualities you would need to accomplish well the mission before you. This is your spiritual end zone. Get it in your sights and run toward it.

*Believe*: Even if you do not believe that you have enough of these qualities on your own, know that God believes you have access to them. How can you be sure? Because God is even less likely than you would ever be to send your children out unprepared and set up to fail. God is in charge of everything. If he is asking you to face something, he knows that you have what it takes to succeed. He believes in you even if you don't. Imagine a version of yourself that already had these qualities. Imagine how this whole, healed, godly, and grace-filled self would respond. Don't imagine some superhero self that doesn't struggle. Instead, imagine how the version of yourself that has these admirable qualities would deal with the negative reactions you often experience in the face of your troubles.

*Lean in*: Finally, lean into this vision of yourself. This is who you really are, the "you" you are becoming. Don't identify with the fallen self you see in the mirror but the authentic you that God's grace makes possible within you. If you have a cold, you don't identify with the cold. You recognize that you are "not yourself" with the cold and can't wait to get over it so that you can "be yourself" again. You recognize that the cold makes you less than what you truly are. It is merely something to be endured and overcome, not something to identify with.

It's the same way with your authentic self. You are not the sinful, broken you. You are infected with vices, sick with sin, afflicted by selfishness and impulsiveness. Sometimes these things might even get to be too much and cause you to be laid up with your spiritual illnesses. But these things are not you. They are merely the diseases God, the Divine Physician, means to deliver you from. Underneath all those spiritual ailments, the real you is cooperating with God's grace to push past the selfishness and sin and emerge victorious and whole—a man after God's own heart (see Acts 13:22).

Be that man. Ask yourself, "How would having these qualities enable me to respond to the challenges I am facing in my life?" Remember, don't imagine some superhero self that never gets irritated, tired, frustrated, or anxious. Imagine the real you, who will probably feel the same way you always do but who can respond to those feelings differently, better, in a more godly way. Write down your goals and review them as you begin each day. Imagine the situations that may occur in the day ahead, and mentally rehearse how you will respond differently. Bring each of these situations to God in prayer, and ask him for the grace to remember your goals and to be able to follow through on them.

At the end of each day, do a mini-examination of conscience. Ask yourself how you did in fulfilling your goal for applying those virtues today. What successes did you have? What challenges did you encounter? What would you need to change to improve upon your progress tomorrow? Write it down and review it the next day in your morning prayer.

### *2. Get a coach.*

You don't win the game on your own. God doesn't need hotshots and show-offs. He needs team players—men who are willing to listen to others and learn from others what they need to do to reach the finish line, men who are willing to be coached. If you are struggling to live out the virtues your present circumstances require of you, get help. Seek peer support, spiritual direction, and, when necessary, faithful counseling. Each plays a different role.

Peer support (men's groups, support groups) provides basic accountability for pursuing your own goals. It can be very useful when you know what your goals are and have the resources to accomplish those goals, but you also need a sympathetic group of like-minded men to support you in achieving your goals. In general, support groups are not supposed to be particularly directive. That is, they don't establish goals for you or teach a lot of skills. They may give you resources, but it is up to you to use them.

Spiritual direction provides basic accountability and support for growing in virtue, going deeper in your relationship with God, and experiencing God more fully in your present circumstances, regardless of whether those circumstances are pleasant or difficult. Your spiritual director can help you establish goals when you aren't sure what you need to do and suggest resources when you are confused about how to achieve those goals. Spiritual direction can involve change, but its main focus is employing spiritual tools to help you encounter Christ more deeply where you are, as you are. It is a long-term relationship focused on long-term spiritual growth and accountability.

Faith-based professional coaching/counseling is primarily focused on change and skill building. It is intended to help you overcome obstacles to success in your life and empower you to transform difficult, dysfunctional situations into healthy ones. A counselor will help you identify the exact nature of your struggles, establish clear goals for overcoming those problems, and teach you specific skills that will enable you to achieve those goals in a more efficient and healthy manner. Counseling tends to be short-term (relatively speaking) and more goal and skill focused than spiritual in nature. You go to counseling to get skills to be stronger, get healthier, and experience greater freedom from the obstacles that hold you back.

Once you are open to the need for regular help to become a man after God's own heart, it is important to get the right kind of help. If you are looking for someone to accompany you on your journey toward God, talk to your pastor about getting regular peer support or spiritual direction. If you are struggling to overcome a particular problem or relationship in your life and feel that the skills you currently have aren't helping you rise to the challenge, it may be time to seek some faithful coaching/counseling.

The point is, we are all men under construction. That doesn't mean God doesn't love you just the way you are. It means that he loves you too much to let you stay that way. He has great plans for your life and fatherhood. Jesus promises you that when you hunger and thirst for righteousness, you will be satisfied. Using the techniques I describe here—among others—can help you be the man God is calling you to be. The man your wife deserves. The man your children need you to be.

## Questions for Reflection

- What difference would it make in your life to begin identifying with your authentic self?
- What qualities would you need to focus on at this stage in your life in order to be more of the man God is calling you to be?
- How would these qualities enable you to respond differently to the challenges you face in your life? Be specific.

- What kind of support do you think you will need (peer support, spiritual direction, faith-based counseling) to successfully practice the qualities you identified as part of your authentic self?

### Prayer

Heavenly Father, I want to be a man after your own heart. Help me to see myself as you see me: whole, healed, godly, and grace-filled. Give me the courage to be the man you know me to be. Satisfy my hunger to be a righteous man who uses every opportunity you give me to grow in strength and virtue and who leads my family to do the same. Amen.

## *Blessed Are the Dads Who Hunger and Thirst for Righteousness*

### Your Relationship with Your Wife

The thirst for righteousness stands at the heart of the mission of Christian marriage. In Ephesians 5:25–28, St. Paul reminds us, "Husbands, love your wives, even as Christ loved the church and handed himself over for her to sanctify her, cleansing her by the bath of water with the word, that he might present to himself the church in splendor, without spot or wrinkle or any such thing, that she might be holy and without blemish. So [also] husbands should love their wives as their own bodies. He who loves his wife loves himself."

What a radical vision this presents! Compare this biblical vision of Christian marriage to the conventional wisdom claiming that the key to a happy marriage is two words: "Yes, dear." Clearly the Ephesians 5 husband is not afraid to lovingly and charitably inspire his wife to discover and lean in to her best self as he takes the lead in welcoming God into every part of the marriage.

As we explored in the chapter on meekness, the godly father does not thirst for righteousness in his marriage by telling his wife how she needs to change to be his version of a better wife and a more godly woman. Rather, he inspires his wife to want to be a better person through his own godly example: by leading couple-prayer, initiating ongoing growth-centered discussions, and looking for ways the marriage can be a more effective sign of God's love. Let's explore each of these in turn:

1. Inspire righteousness by example.
2. Lead couple-prayer.
3. Encourage your wife's mission.
4. Creat a marital mission.

### *1. Inspire righteousness by example.*

The husband who is leaning in to his best self (as we discussed in the first section of this chapter) does not put on airs or try to act better than he is, but he regularly strives to be better than he is. In doing so, he invites his wife to be a partner with him in creating a godlier home by becoming better, godlier people.

Such a husband asks his wife what she would need from him to feel like he was putting her first, and then he does those things without having to be asked again. He actively looks for ways to make his wife's life easier or more pleasant, surprising her with simple acts of kindness that lighten her load or brighter her day—"just because." He doesn't keep score or refuse to give more than he gets. Instead, he serves generously, and while he doesn't allow himself to be used as an object (a beast of burden), he gently addresses any concerns he may have, being careful not to lecture or shame her but asking her to join him in serving each other and the marriage as best as they can. He leads couple-prayer and asks God to bless their marriage and use it to make them holy.

Such a husband is a true inspiration to his wife. This is a man who does not beg to be followed but neither does he keep his head down and try to stay out of the way. He leads by example, by not counting the cost, because he knows that is what God asks of him. He presents himself as a man who is willing to listen and happy to lead—as long as he is leading the family into deeper intimacy in the home and helping the family become a more faithful sign of God's love in the world.

### *2. Lead couple-prayer.*

We discussed couple-prayer in general in the chapter on the second BeDADitude. Here I want to discuss the importance of not just willingly participating in couple-prayer but initiating it as well. Christian husbands should not wait for their wives to remind them that it is time to pray. The man who hungers and thirsts for righteousness is committed to bringing his spouse to Christ every day. He takes the lead in blessing her in the morning, initiating a brief prayer over their day. This could be as simple as laying hands on her and saying, "Lord, bless my wife, and help her to glorify you in everything she does today," or as involved as leading a more extensive morning prayer time using the PRAISE format we discussed earlier. He takes the lead in saying grace and giving thanks to God for all they have been given. He takes the lead in initiating prayers of some sort before they go to bed so that they can bring their day to God, give thanks for their blessings, and ask for God's assistance to be ever more faithful the next day.

Such a husband knows that he and his beloved cannot become righteous through their own power, so he looks for opportunities to sit with his bride in the presence of Righteousness himself.

### *3. Encourage your wife's mission.*

Earlier in this chapter, you reflected on what your best self looks like. That is, you identified the virtues that represent your whole, healed, godly, grace-filled self. These qualities, when referred to consistently, become your polestar and compass to guide your decision-making and priority setting. Having this list of virtues gives you a sense of mission and makes your quest to use the challenges of everyday life to grow in virtue a possible task.

It will be important to lead your wife through a similar exercise. It doesn't have to be a formal process. Let it take whatever shape she feels comfortable with. Simply lead your wife in a conversation about the kind of people you feel God is calling you to become. Ask her who she imagines herself to be when she is her real-life "best self." Not some imaginary superhero self who never has problems or struggles, but the person who handles these struggles with grace. What are the qualities she would possess if she could be this person? Ask her how you can best support her in being this person. Be careful not to lecture her or criticize her when she struggles to live up to these standards. Instead, be helpful. If you see her struggling with anger, frustration, a lack of confidence, or any other thing that is making her all too aware of her limitations, simply take her in your arms and lovingly say something like, "You seem like you're really having a tough time connecting with the woman I know you really are. What can I do to help you find that awesome, godly, grace-filled woman again?"

Every wife longs for a man who can help her become the woman she wants to be without belittlement or criticism. When you show her that you know who she is when she is at her best and that you are committed to doing what you can to help her close the gap between the person she is being in the moment and the person she would like to be, you will earn her deep respect and admiration. Help your wife discover and live her mission. Be the Ephesians 5 husband who presents his wife to Christ as the spotless bride she is called to be by loving her, serving her, and supporting her in her efforts to let God's grace bring out her best self in every moment of everyday life. This is the essence of true Christian headship: helping your wife become the woman God created her to be by offering her your loving support and service.

### *4. Create a marital mission.*

God brought you and your wife together not only to love and support each other but to bear witness to his face in the world. God is too big, too awesome, too wonderful for any one person to represent him completely. That's why he brings people together to create religious communities and families, to reveal different aspects of himself to the world. We're used to thinking of religious communities this way. We all know that certain orders of priests are teachers, while others are preachers, and still others have different charisms altogether. But charisms like this are not just for the ordained and religious. Couples and families have charisms—ministries that build up the body of Christ and show God's love to the world. Do you know what the charism of your marriage is?

Some couples have the gift of hospitality. They do a wonderful job making people feel loved by welcoming them into their homes and sharing their lives. Other couples have the gift of a particular kind of service. They feel drawn to serve in particular parish ministries or community outreaches. Other couples have a particular heart for children and create large families or find ways to be spiritual parents to children in need. Other couples are called to other charisms.

Talk with your wife about the good God wants to do in the world through your marriage. Don't make this more complicated than it has to be. Simply reflect on the things you enjoy doing as a couple—the hobbies, passions, or interests you have—and ask how you might work together and use those hobbies, passions, or interests to bless the Body of Christ. Are you gardeners? Can you share what you grow with the local soup kitchen? Are you musicians? Can you volunteer in your parish music ministry or give concerts at the local nursing home? What gifts or interest do you and your spouse have, and how can you put those gifts and interests at the service of the people around you? God wants to bless the world through your marriage. Work together with your wife to discover what a blessing the two of you are—not just to each other but to your parish and community as well.

## Questions for Reflection

- In what concrete ways would you like to do a better job loving and serving your wife in your day-to-day relationship with her?
- What things can you do to become more confident leading couple-prayer with your wife?
- How could you do a better job encouraging your wife to be her best self without resorting to criticism or lecturing?
- What ways could you and your wife work together to be a blessing to your parish or community?

Thirsting for righteousness compels the Catholic father to actively look for ways his home can be a blessing to those who dwell within and without its walls. By being a model of Christ's love in the home—leading your wife to an encounter with God through couple-prayer, supporting your wife in being her best self, and looking for ways to make your marriage a blessing to the world—you are tapping the root of righteousness in your home and allowing your marriage to be a conduit of grace.

## Prayer

Heavenly Father, help me thirst for righteousness in my marriage. Give me the grace I need to be a model of virtuous, loving service in my home. Help me find the courage to lead my wife to encounter you more deeply in our couple-prayer times. Enable me to bring out the best in my wife through my loving and generous support, and help my wife and I discover your plans for blessing the world through our relationship. Amen.

## *Blessed Are the Dads Who Hunger and Thirst for Righteousness*

### Your Relationship with Your Children

There is no greater joy than raising truly godly children. The entire point of Christian family life is raising young men and women who can raise the bar in all they do and bring the world to Christ. Our children belong to God. They are simply on loan to us for a time. It is our greatest duty and privilege as Christian fathers to raise children to love God with all their hearts, minds, souls, and strength and live lives of Christian zeal.

This kind of passion for the kingdom does not just happen. We have to teach our children that God has great plans for their lives from the time that they are little to the time that they are full-grown adults. Fathers play a critical role in making this happen. Following the Holocaust, research was done to determine why some people collaborated with the Nazi persecution of the Jews (or merely stood by while it happened) while others courageously rescued the Jews at great personal risk. The difference had nothing to do with religious involvement, political affiliation, educational attainment, or socioeconomic status. So what gave rescuers the courage to resist the sociopolitical tide of Jewish persecution? Rescuers alone were raised in households where fathers took the lead in their character formation. Furthermore, fathers of rescuers used gentle methods of correction that avoided heavy-handed punishments in favor of encouraging virtue and talking children through the consequences of their actions.

The more heavy-handed the father's discipline, the more likely it was that the adult children would be collaborators with the Nazis because they were not taught to distinguish between good and bad authority; they were merely taught to be obedient. Likewise, children whose mothers were primarily responsible for character development seemed to struggle with applying the lessons they learned in the world. They may have felt that the systematic persecution of the Jews was wrong, but they could not bring themselves to do anything about it. Only those young men and women raised by fathers who hungered and thirsted for justice in their homes raised children who were courageous enough to be Christian heroes. And they did it by refusing to settle for mere obedience, instead preferring to teach their children how to think about their actions and make virtuous choices regardless of the cost.

Subsequent research has shown that children of faithful fathers are almost fifteen times more likely to be faithful as adults—even if their mothers are unchurched—than children raised in households with a faithful mother and an unchurched father.

Why are fathers so important? For the first months after birth, the baby thinks of the mother as merely an extension of his own body. This makes sense. The child was actually part of the mother's body for nine months. The child does not even have the mental capacity to begin working out that he is a separate being from his mother until at least sixteen months of age and does not fully individuate until he is approaching his third year of life. As such, the father represents the child's "first other." If the mother is, symbolically, self and home, the father is, symbolically, "the world." If the mother is faithful, the child recognizes that faith should be practiced privately, in the realm of existence closest to himself. But if the child's father is genuinely faithful, the child comes to believe that faith must be lived out loud in "the world." The fact that so many Catholics believe that faith and prayer are "too private" to be shared openly is a direct indictment of the absence of generations of godly Catholic fathers.

Let this satanic culture of spiritual fatherlessness end with you. Resolve to stop the cycle where spiritually fatherless Catholic families are satisfied to raise half-hearted, passively faithful kids who fall away and fumble around in the darkness of young adulthood until they have their own kids and repeat the process, mindlessly raising the next generation of spiritually fatherless, lukewarm Catholics. Let your home be the place that passionately faithful, prayerful, godly children are raised. Let your hunger and thirst for righteousness empower you to be that man.

1. Teach your kids to pray.
2. Challenge them to raise the bar.
3. Teach them their mission.
4. Encourage their charisms.

## *1. Teach your kids to pray.*

As you know by now, we can only be righteous to the degree that we are standing as close as possible to the source of righteousness himself, that is, God. Show your children the way. Lead meaningful family prayer. Pray over your children. Before they go to school, before they have a game, before they take that test, before they go to bed, lay your hand on their heads and bless them: "Lord, bless my child. Let him discover all the amazing gifts you have given him, and let him use those gifts to be a blessing to others, to do great things, to glorify you, and to lead everyone he meets to a closer relationship with you."

In addition to leading prayer with your children, teach your children to pray. Ask them to lead family prayer, and coach them through the process (using the PRAISE format). Teach them to talk to God throughout the day, thanking him for the good things, asking for help with the struggles. When you are hugging your children, remind them how much you love them and that the only person who loves them more is God. Talk about God openly in your home. Share stories of answered prayers. Lead prayers expressing the needs of the household. During family prayer, prompt the children to pray aloud about the things you know are on their hearts. Let your kids see you taking regular time for personal prayer, and help them carve out time in their day for at least a few minutes of their own prayer times. To thirst for righteousness is to thirst for God. Teach your children to drink from the stream of Living Water that is his Divine Presence. If you feel insecure about how to accomplish any of this, read *Discovering God Together: The Catholic Guide to Raising Faithful Kids*. It can help you develop the confidence you need to raise truly godly children.

## Questions for Reflection

- How do you pray with your children now?
- What more could you do to model meaningful prayer to your children?
- How could you do more to lead your children to have their own relationships with God?

### *2. Challenge them to raise the bar.*

Remind your children that wherever they go and whatever they do, God asks them to be faithful leaders. The point is not to nag, lecture, shame, or harangue your children. The goal is not to be a religious helicopter killjoy father. The goal is to seek gentle ways to lovingly encourage your kids to be their best selves and bring out the best in others as well. This begins at home.

Remind your children to encourage their brothers and sisters to do their chores, prompt one another to be respectful, take turns, and care for one another. Praise them when they remember to do this; gently remind them when they forget. Insist that older children model good behavior for younger ones. Praise them when they do; impose gentle consequences when they forget. When your children do something particularly kind or generous, celebrate it as a family with extra affection, a special family activity, or a special treat. If a child is disobedient or disrespectful and a brother or sister encouraged, aided, or abetted the misbehavior, they should both share in the consequences. Your family sinks or swims together. Remind your children that you expect them to encourage each other to do what is good and right.

Once you have established this dynamic in your home, it's time to take the show on the road. We have always had a deal with our children that we would not restrict who they played with as long as we saw them taking the lead in encouraging healthy play, good behavior, and appropriate language. We would praise our children on the way home from playdates when we saw them refusing to play inappropriately and instead suggesting positive games. We would observe our children when they struggled to do this, and, when we got home, we would role-play godly ways to manage these scenarios the next time they came up. We also reminded our children that if they came home from spending time with friends or doing some activities and we saw that they allowed those experiences to negatively impact their language or their behavior, they would not be allowed to go with those friends or engage in those activities again until they cleaned up their act and got those influences out of their system. As a Christian father, I do not see it as my role to hide my children from the world but to teach them to engage it in a faithful, godly manner.

Our children are going to be exposed to many things that are both outside our control and contrary to the Gospel. That is not a problem as long as they know how to handle themselves. It is the godly father's job to teach them how to do this by making sure that they are mature enough to influence their world—and avoid the alternative. By encouraging them to raise the bar wherever they are, supporting them in doing so whenever we see them struggling, and refusing to allow them to participate in anything they show us they can't handle without guidance, they will learn that they have an obligation, as children of God, to try to leave every person and every situation better than they found it. When this costs them in some way, be there to console them, comfort them, and praise them for their heroic witness. It is in these times in particular that we must be most proud of them.

## Questions for Reflection

- What opportunities do your children have to be Christian witnesses to their siblings and peers?
- How do you currently talk to them about the ways they bring Christ to others?
- What more could you do to encourage your children to be godly leaders with their friends and in all the situations they find themselves?

## *3. Teach them their mission.*

Encourage your children to be their best selves by asking them what virtues they most wish to be known for. If they were starring in their own reality TV shows how would viewers describe them? As flaky? Selfish? Helpful? Generous? Whether we know it or not, the choices we make broadcast a message to the world. God wants us to manage that message so that our lives proclaim his love, his truth, his light. Ask your children what qualities they most want to be known for, and ask them to regularly reflect on their own behavior in light of those virtues. Don't scold them when they misbehave. Hold up a mirror. If a child who says she wants to be a loving person acts disrespectfully, say, "Sweetheart, you've told me that you want to be thought of as a loving person. Do you think speaking to me that way serves that goal?" When your child struggles to answer, say, "Then please try that again in a more loving way, and I promise to listen." When your child who wishes to be a champion does a halfhearted job on his homework, say, "You've said that you want to be thought of as a champion, a young man who isn't afraid to do hard things to win the race. Tell me honestly—does this look like the work of a champion?" When your child shrugs and looks embarrassed, say, "It's OK. Everyone drops the ball once in a while. A champion picks it up and tries again. Give this another go." Children as young as six can respond well to this type of questioning. With younger children you can take a similar approach, but you will need to teach rather than question. For instance, say, "Honey, in this family, we all try to be loving people. Loving people do not speak that way. Please say that again in a loving way." Then help them find the words and tone of voice that matches.

This approach teaches your children to internalize their values and reflect on their own behavior in light of those values instead of waiting around for you to tell them how little they can get away with. Rather than teaching children to jump through your hoops, you are encouraging your children to develop their own strong moral consciences and personal integrity. My wife and I discuss this powerful discipline technique—along with many other strategies for godly discipline—in *Parenting with Grace*, but for now, it is enough to remember that discipline isn't just about getting your children to obey. It is ultimately about getting your kids to be people of character. This requires helping them realize who they really are (i.e., people of virtue) and how their behavior from moment to moment impacts their ability to live up to that mission.

## Questions for Reflection

- Does your approach to discipline simply focus on compliance, or are you actively teaching your children how to own their values and make good choices even when you aren't around to enforce virtuous conduct?

- How will you do more to encourage your children to be authentically virtuous people—not just in their behavior but in their hearts?

## *4. Encourage their charisms.*

God has given every child certain gifts or talents. Some children's gifts are more obvious than others, but all children have them, and it is our job as fathers who thirst for righteousness to not only teach our children how to discover and hone their gifts but to place them in service of the Lord and his people.

Begin by encouraging service in the home. Children as young as three love to help around the house. Find little ways to let them. Create the expectation from the earliest ages that Christians discover their true selves by using whatever they have to work for the good of others.

Beyond this, as your children begin to show more specific talents and personality traits, lead them in conversation about how they can use those gifts to bless others and build up the Body of Christ. Make sure to drill your athletes in good sportsmanship on and off the field (and make sure you model such behavior at their games). If your children are musical, get them involved in the parish music ministry. Does your child have a big heart? Suggest an age-appropriate social justice project he or she could become involved in at the parish or in the community. Is your child known for his strength? Encourage him to use that strength to help those who are not as strong and to stand up for the kids being picked on at school. Is your child a good organizer? Let her volunteer to help arrange books at the parish library or goods at the local food-distribution center. Whatever your child's gifts are, encourage him or her to use those gifts to be a blessing to others. As your child grows, teach him or her about charisms—those gifts God gives us to reveal his presence in the world and to use for other's good. While you're at it, make sure to look for opportunities to serve your parish or community together as a family. The website www.DoingGoodTogether.org has many ideas for how families can serve their communities together.

## Questions for Reflection

- In what ways does your family work together to serve your parish or community (not individually but as a group)?
- What gifts (talents or strengths) do your children have? How do you encourage them to use these strengths and talents for the good of God's kingdom?
- What more could you do to encourage your children to use their whole selves to work for the good of those around them—both inside and outside the home?

The family is the basic unit of civilization. The best way for a Christian father to build the kingdom is to (a) lead his family to Christ; (b) create a righteous family life by encouraging a spirit of generous, mutual self-giving; and (c) share the gift of your family with the wider community through Christian service.

In the fourth Beatitude, Jesus says that those who hunger and thirst for righteousness will be satisfied. There is nothing as satisfying for a godly father than watching his children mature in their relationships with God and discover together all the ways they can use their gifts to bless each other and the world. The energy you spend to create a righteous family is never wasted. Let your family bear witness to all the good that God can do in and through families when godly fathers are actively engaged in bringing the people that depend upon them to Christ.

## Prayer

Heavenly Father, I hunger and thirst to lead a righteous family. Help me to see myself through your eyes and enable my wife and children to see themselves through your eyes in turn. Help me to lead my family to have a deep and meaningful relationship with you. Teach me how to inspire my wife and children to develop all their gifts to the fullest and use them to build up our household and your people as a whole. Satisfy my hunger for a righteous heart, a righteous home, and a righteous world. Amen.

# THE FIFTH BeDADitude

## Blessed are the dads who are merciful. They will be shown mercy.

What does it truly mean to be merciful? There is a popular perception that being merciful means letting someone off the hook, but, while there is a sense in which this is true, mercy means so much more.

Consider, for example, the Corporal and Spiritual Works of Mercy.

The Corporal Works of Mercy are listed as follows:

1. Feed the hungry.
2. Give drink to the thirsty.
3. Clothe the naked.
4. Give shelter to the homeless.
5. Visit the sick.
6. Visit the imprisoned.
7. Bury the dead.

The Spiritual Works of Mercy are listed below:

1. Instruct the ignorant.
2. Counsel the doubtful.
3. Admonish sinners.
4. Bear wrongs patiently.
5. Forgive offenses willingly.
6. Comfort the afflicted.
7. Pray for the living and the dead.

Although it does not occur to many people, these works of mercy give us an operational definition of what it means to actually be merciful. Taken at face value, they can seem like just random ways we could be nice to people. In fact, on that superficial level, these lists can even seem contradictory. For instance, how is it merciful to both forgive willingly and admonish sinners? The key to understanding how these lists define mercy is asking, "What do these lists have in common?" When you apply this question, the actual definition of mercy becomes clear. To be merciful is to treat others in a manner that demonstrates their worth in the eyes of God.

We engage in works of mercy such as clothing the naked because every child of God deserves to be dressed in a manner that reveals his or her dignity as a son or daughter of the King of kings! We feed the hungry because every person deserves to know that he or she has a rightful place at the royal feast set at God's table! We forgive willingly and bear wrongs patiently because we recognize the challenges involved in becoming saints and because we try to be generous about the struggle that's part of that process. And yet, when those we love forget who they really are, neglect to strive for greatness, and, instead, decide to wallow in their brokenness, we admonish them, not to condemn or judge but to invite them to remember that they were meant to be more and to live more fully than they are. (Note: *The Corporal Works of Mommy [and Daddy Too]* explores how the various works of mercy can enable you to view even the most mundane tasks of family life as a powerful path to holiness.)

Returning to our discussion of the fifth BeDADitude, the father who is merciful is committed to remembering who he is as a son of God and approaching all the tasks of fathering and family life in a manner that reminds his wife and children what they are worth in God's eyes.

## *Blessed Are the Dads Who Are Merciful*

### Your Relationship with God

In our chapter on the second BeDADitude ("Blessed are the dads who mourn"), we looked at the importance of having compassion for ourselves in our weaknesses and failings. When we explored the fourth BeDADitude ("Blessed are the dads who hunger and thirst for righteousness"), we discovered our true identities as sons of God. As we reflect on the idea of being merciful to ourselves in our relationships with God, it is time to consider how to cooperate with God's desire to transform us from the inside out into new creations. We will explore what it means to live out the command of Ephesians 4:24 and "put on the new [man], created in God's way in righteousness and holiness of truth."

There is a saying that "God loves us just the way we are, but he loves us too much to let us stay that way." Just as you love your children for who they are today while simultaneously knowing that they are destined for so much more, your heavenly Father loves you for who you are but calls you to a greatness beyond your wildest dreams—divine sonship. God wants to make you—a mortal, sinful being—into a new man who will be perfected in Christ, capable of living forever and destined to being united with God's infinite love for all eternity. He wants nothing less than to make us "share in the divine nature" (2 Pt 1:4).

Many of us have been taught that the primary mission of the Christian is to be constantly on guard against sin. It is not. The Christian is defined not by what he runs from but rather by whom he runs to! Yes, of course, we must change if we are going to become the "new men" we are meant to be, but we cannot approach this change in the same old way. How many times have you tried to change something about yourself only to find that you keep falling into the same hole over and over again? As we have already discussed in an earlier chapter, this is because we fuel our attempts to change with the inferior fuel of self-hatred, condemnation, and criticism. New men need new fuel, mined from mercy and packed with all the potential energy needed to help us become true sons of God.

## *New fuel for new men.*

In his theology of the body, St. John Paul II teaches us that by reflecting on the design of our bodies, we can discover important truths about God's intention for our lives and relationships. What do our bodies say about the best way of cooperating with God's plan for our perfection? Surprisingly, it teaches us that the need for mercy is hardwired into the brain's capacity for godly change.

In order for us to make lasting change in our lives, our brains need to be able to rewire themselves. New neural pathways need to be formed, and sometimes new nerve cells need to be grown. That's why change can feel like such hard work. You are literally trying to rewire your brain and change your brain chemistry just by changing your thoughts and habits. UCLA psychiatrist and brain researcher Dr. Daniel Siegel discovered that self-criticism and self-condemnation actually stalls the process of protein synthesis in the brain that allows new neural pathways to be formed. The chemicals associated with the psychological process of self-criticism cause the brain to go into a physiological lockdown mode as the brain detects a threat and redirects all energy to preserving existing neural networks. The chemicals that lock your brain in place also stop the process by which new learning takes root on the neurological level. That means the more you beat up on yourself, the more intractable your ungodly behavior becomes.

Siegel—who, in addition to his groundbreaking work in interpersonal neurobiology (the science of how relationships affect brain development), has served as a scientific consultant to the Vatican's Pontifical Council for the Family—also observed that there are four specific qualities that produce a rich neurochemical fertilizer of sorts in the brain that greatly enhances neuroplasticity, the brain's ability to rewire itself and grow new healthy connections that support new, healthy change. Represented by the acronym COAL, these qualities are listed as follows:

1. Curiosity
2. Openness
3. Acceptance
4. Love

In my book *Broken Gods: Hope, Healing, and the Seven Longings of the Human Heart*, I fully develop the ways that COAL can fuel our ability to cooperate with God's plan for our ultimate fulfillment. Here is a brief treatment of how COAL can help make it easier for us to become the men, the husbands, and the fathers God is calling us to be without resorting to the self-criticism and self-hatred that we commonly indulge in, in an attempt to create change in our lives.

### *1. Curiosity*

Curiosity is the opposite of the denial that results from self-condemnation. Usually when we let ourselves, our wives, or our kids down in some way, we respond by beating up on ourselves. As a result, we work overtime to ignore the problem—or worse, deny it—which makes cooperating with the grace God gives us to change impossible. Curiosity allows us to look more closely at the wound that is driving the perceived failure. It allows us to ask, "What work must I allow God to do in me? What must be healed in order for me to be more of the man/husband/father I am being called to become?" It takes courage to ask these questions, but the courage curiosity requires makes authentic change possible.

## *2. Openness*

Openness is the quality that allows us to accept the answers our curiosity provides. Too often, even when we find the courage to ask hard questions about the wounds that underlie our struggles, we become frightened by what we discover. We gain insights but immediately dismiss them: "That couldn't possibly have anything to do with this." "That's ancient history. I should be over that!" "That's ridiculous. Why should something like that still bother me? It's stupid!" Openness is the quality that allows me to prayerfully reflect upon the answers my curiosity reveals. True, some of my insights might be more accurate than others, but I won't be able to make that determination until I bring all of my insights to prayer and reflect on them in the light of God's grace. Finding the courage to first look more closely at the reasons behind my struggles and then reflect upon the nature of those wounds allows me to see exactly where I need the most grace, the most healing, and how, specifically, to cooperate with the work God wants to do in me.

## *3. Acceptance*

Acceptance allows me to be patient with the work God is doing in me. When we discover problems, our natural tendency is to want to run around fixing them immediately. It doesn't matter whether those "fixes" are permanent. Too often, we're willing to settle for patches and work-arounds. We don't really want to heal. We want to compensate so that we can go back to pretending that we are perfect just the way we are. For instance, we say,

> "Who, me? Struggle with porn? Ridiculous. I'm just not going to look at it anymore. See? Now I have a computer filter. Problem solved!"
>
> "Sure, I used to have a temper, but now I have it under control. These days I just totally shut down when I get angry. I never complain about anything. Everything's fine!"
>
> "I know, I know, I work too much. I just have to get my priorities straight. As soon as this big project is done, I'll rework my schedule. I've totally got this."

We may be happy with temporary fixes, patches, and work-arounds, but God wants more for his sons. He desires—no, he demands—that we be willing to undertake total transformation. This transformation takes time, effort, persistence, grace, and, above all, patience. Patience, by the way, is not a passive quality. It is the active process of observing the effect our efforts have made and plotting the next step. It is the opposite of hammering away at something over and over again despite the fact that everything I am doing is just making things worse. Acceptance is the willingness to see that, while we have our part to do, ultimately we must be patient and accept the process God is working in us. Acceptance allows us to both believe and submit to the idea that God's grace is sufficient and that in our weakness God can reveal his glory (see 2 Cor 12:9–10).

### *4. Love*

Finally, love allows us to commit to the effort it requires to persistently work for our own good, growth, and development. We tend to think of self-improvement as women's work. Men don't need to grow. We just need a beer. Or a nap. Or more sex. We're fine neglecting ourselves if we are just given permission to numb out in the process.

Jesus commanded us to do more than numb out. He commanded us to love our neighbors as we love ourselves. True Christian love of self is not self-indulgent or smarmy. It is tough. It sees what we can be, what God wants to make us—whole, healed, godly, and grace-filled sons of the Father—and it compels us to "begin building" (see Neh 2:18). True Christian love of self is unconditional, not in the sense that it allows us to indulge in whatever damn fool thing we feel like doing but in the sense that it commits us to working with God to complete his work in us whether we feel like it or not, whether we think we deserve it or not, whether we want to or not. True love of self represents the commitment to see to our total growth and development as sons of God so that he may be glorified in us. In the words of the soldier-saint Ignatius of Loyola, *Ad majorem Dei gloriam*—"Let everything I do be to the greater glory of God!"

Can you see the radical difference that COAL fuels in our lives? As research by UCLA's Center for Culture, Brain, Development, and Mental Health shows, COAL enables psychological and spiritual change to become firmly rooted in the biological processes of the mind that make transformation permanent and real. COAL is a catalyst for the process God created in the brain to allow certain chemicals to be produced, permitting neuroplasticity and embodied, godly change to occur. COAL is the heart of mercy directed toward oneself. It allows us to remind ourselves of who we truly are in God's eyes while simultaneously enabling us to free ourselves from the trap of perpetual failure and self-hatred and make peace with the work God is doing in us in his perfect time.

To become men after God's own heart, we have to begin by viewing ourselves with God's own merciful eyes, loving ourselves for both what we are and what we are destined to become through God's grace and abundant mercy.

### Questions for Reflection

- When are you most prone to self-criticism, self-condemnation, or self-hatred?
- What difference would it make to use COAL to fuel the changes you need to make in these areas of your life?

### Prayer

Heavenly Father, I praise you for your mercy. Help me to remember my worth in your eyes and the work you are doing in me. Give me the power to stop criticizing myself, to stop settling for imperfect patches, "fixes," and workarounds, and instead to embrace the deep change you want to work in me. Give me the courage to embrace the new creation you want me to be, and let me fuel my ability to cooperate with your grace in a spirit of curiosity, openness, acceptance, and love so that that changes you work in me can be bone-deep and lasting. Amen.

## *Blessed Are the Dads Who Are Merciful*

### Your Relationship with Your Wife

Jesus reminds us that the key to receiving mercy is being merciful to others. The process just reviewed of extending mercy to yourself becomes much simpler if you have created a marriage and family life rooted in mercy. Of course, this begins by practicing mercy in your marriage. Here are ways you can begin doing this today:

1. Be demonstrative with your love.
2. Serve with joy.
3. Bear wrongs patiently, and forgive willingly.

### *1. Be demonstrative with your love.*

Remember, to be merciful is to treat others in a manner that reminds them of their worth in God's eyes. The Corporal and Spiritual Works of Mercy are just different examples of ways that we can do this, but it all begins not with a begrudging willingness to perform certain tasks for the good of others but with a deep passionate love for those around us.

Many men have been raised to believe that it is somehow unseemly—if not downright unmanly—to be demonstrative with love and affection. This is a myth. In many cultures throughout the world, men are as demonstrative of affection and emotion as women. In some cases, more so. In fact, returning to the theology of the body, brain science teaches us that when boys are raised properly in healthy, affectionate homes, they naturally develop a strong ability to be empathic, nurturing, and demonstrative of affection in a way that is profoundly affirming and not at all effeminate. The fact that we in the West assume that it is normal for men to struggle in this regard is deeply disturbing considering that we now know that the struggle to be emotionally and affectionately demonstrative is actually a disorder psychologists refer to as avoidant attachment. The disorder is rooted in underdeveloped structures of the social brain caused by emotionally impoverished parenting, the effects of which can be seen using current brain-imaging technology.

The point is, every man was created by God to have the capacity to be fully emotional, affectionately demonstrative, and empathic—just as the heavenly Father is with us. If this does not describe you then, at some point, your true masculine inheritance was stolen from you, and it is time to reclaim what is yours. The best way to do this is by being affectionate, both physically (through nonsexual hugs, cuddling, etc.) and emotionally (by giving meaningful compliments and listening attentively). The trick, however, is resisting the temptation of seeing physical and emotional affection as the means to a sexual end. In the popular imagination, men have a reputation for being unable to be affectionate without it necessarily leading to sex, but in truth we are also seeing this trait more and more in millennial women, who are quite sexually aggressive. Why? Because the detached, unaffectionate way boys were historically parented has now become the norm for girls as well. Again, this inability to be affectionate without turning it into a sexual overture has been considered by many to be part and parcel of the male experience, but as attachment research—supported by the real-life examples of behavior of contemporary young women—shows, this trait is merely the result of insufficient affection and bonding in childhood. The good news is that men who struggle with this deficit can learn to reclaim the godly inheritance of being selflessly affectionate by determined practice. Look for opportunities to hug your wife, hold her in your arms, sit with her on the couch, and otherwise minister to her body without turning these into sexual overtures. The same goes for emotional affection. Give her specific compliments about her appearance, notice and comment on the nice things she does for you, thank her for the service she provides to you and the family—especially if it is just part of her "job." Tell her when she does things that please you, and make sure to actively look for those things. Catch her being good. Show her worth in God's eyes by being present and being affectionate.

## Questions for Reflection

- What is your experience of being affectionate without it necessarily leading to sex? How could you do a better job of physically showing your wife what she is worth without expecting to be "compensated" for your efforts?
- If you were going to be more physically affectionate and complimentary, where would you start?

- When you listen well at work or with friends, how do you act? How is this different from the way you listen to your wife? If you were going to be a better listener with your wife, what would you need to do differently?

## *2. Serve with joy.*

Remember the Corporal Works of Mercy, and serve your wife. Folding laundry even when you aren't asked is a wonderful way to practice clothing the naked in your home. Making a meal (and not just the one meal you learned to cook in college so you wouldn't starve) or volunteering to do the dishes are terrific ways to practice feeding the hungry. Leaving the room you were just in a little cleaner or neater than you found it is an excellent way to practice truly sheltering those in your home. My wife and I wrote about these little acts of service in *The Corporal Works of Mommy (and Daddy Too)*. They can be a powerful spiritual exercise, especially when you do these things joyfully.

Of course, when she actually asks you to do something, don't just say, "Yes, dear." Follow through without being reminded. Be diligent and cheerful about the opportunities God gives you to serve your family. No, you won't always feel like it, and sometimes you might need a break. It's OK to take care of yourself too, but resist the feeling that you've done your bit simply by going to work that day. Yes, that work was an important gift to your family, but it can't end there. Don't miss out on the 1,001 other ways to serve them directly. Remember, mercy means treating others in a way that reminds them of their worth in God's eyes. Unfortunately, work often takes us away from our families, and, if we aren't careful about our approach to work, the time we spend on our jobs can sometimes communicate that we value our work more than our families at home. Saving at least some energy for serving around the house helps your family remember how precious they are to you because you had to keep them in mind all day to reserve the energy you are spending on them once you got home.

In a similar vein, don't make your wife remind you to do the things she has asked you to do. Put reminders in your phone. If you give her your word, let it be your bond. Treat her requests as the most important thing you have to do—because, as she is the only person (besides your children) God himself has given you to care for, they are.

Finally, resist the temptation to resentfully wonder why you should have to do anything if she was doing her job. It doesn't matter that many men know that they aren't "supposed" to treat home care and childcare as women's work; many of us still display this attitude in practice. Of course, if in the process of genuinely working hard to serve your wife and be her partner in caring for your children and home you somehow feel like you are being taken advantage of, it is perfectly acceptable to discuss ways to address your concerns. But if you find you have to raise the issue, take a moment, pray about what you want to say, and then say it gently and helpfully. "Hon, can you think of any way we could do a better job working together to get everything done?" will yield a much different response than, "You know, if you just did your job I wouldn't have to spend so much energy picking up your slack."

Serving generously and reliably and addressing concerns respectfully are all ways you can show your wife what she is worth to God and to you.

## Questions for Reflection

- Think of the Corporal and Spiritual Works of Mercy listed at the beginning of this chapter. In what specific ways could you do a better job taking advantage of opportunities to serve your wife by practicing the various works of mercy at home? What kind of help would she most appreciate?

- Do you tend to feel resentful about the things you "have" to do to help your wife? How could you either challenge your selfishness or address concerns respectfully so that you could take the lead in creating a better partnership with your wife?

## *3. Bear wrongs patiently, and forgive willingly.*

Of course, one of the most obvious ways to be merciful in your marriage is to practice the Spiritual Works of Mercy: bear wrongs patiently, and forgive willingly. Many men are afraid to do these things in their marriages because they are certain that they require them to be passive patsies.

Bearing wrongs patiently is actually a very active process that protects your dignity and the dignity of the wrongdoer—in this case, your wife. As I show in my book *Broken Gods: Hope, Healing, and the Seven Longings of the Human Heart,* patience is not the passive act of merely "lying down and taking it." Rather, it reminds us that wrongs require a thoughtful, measured response. Patience is the virtue that allows me to observe what the best way to respond to something is and to consider whether my response is having the effect I was hoping for. If not, patience allows me to step back and consider my next step. The opposite of responding patiently is responding reactively, either by shutting down and pouting about the slight or letting loose and having a tantrum about it. Your relationship deserves better than this. Let your marriage be blessed by the mercy that is extended when you either consciously and thoughtfully decide that something is genuinely not worth making a fuss about or when you consciously and thoughtfully decide to address a problem with respect and kindness.

In a similar way, forgiving willingly is not the "virtue" of passively sucking it up. St. Augustine taught that forgiveness is simply the act of surrendering your desire for revenge. In marriage, forgiving willingly means refusing to create drama by lashing out or getting back at your wife when she does something to offend you. Forgiving does not stop you from addressing the offense; it is actually the first step to addressing the problem respectfully. Forgiveness, in the truest sense of the word, enables our reactive anger to drain away so that we can address problems appropriately and proportionately and find answers that truly meet our marriages' needs.

When we bear marital wrongs patiently and forgive our wives willingly, we model the self-control and respect that enables us to take the lead finding respectful solutions to marital problems. True leadership always shines in crisis. Practicing mercy in our marriages allows us to pilot our relationships through the storms of life and find the safe harbor of mutually satisfying solutions that creates true peace and harmony in our homes.

## Questions for Reflection

- Do the definitions of bearing wrongs patiently and forgiving willingly you read here differ from your previous understanding of these works of mercy? If so, how?
- What wrongs do you have a hard time bearing patiently or forgiving willingly (and instead respond to with pouting or having a tantrum)? How might you approach these situations differently in the future, knowing the real meaning of these works of mercy?

## Prayer

Heavenly Father, thank you for all the opportunities you give me to learn mercy with my wife. You have shown me abundant mercy, and I thank you for the opportunity to share that mercy with the woman I love most in the world. Help me to affirm her willingly, serve her generously and cheerfully, and forgive her graciously in ways that lead to more peace in our home. Amen.

## ***Blessed Are the Dads Who Are Merciful***

### Your Relationship with Your Children

As I noted in the introduction to our discussion on marriage, our ability to receive God's mercy is dependent upon the mercy we show to the people who share our lives. Jesus reminds us that children in particular are precious to God's heart and have a special claim to both his and our mercy as their guardian angels sit closest to the Father, interceding before him on their behalf. "See that you do not despise one of these little ones, for I say to you that their angels in heaven always look upon the face of my heavenly Father" (Mt 18:10). The following are simple ways we can show the Father's mercy to our children and remind them of their worth in God's eyes and in our own:

1. Show 'em you care through affection and service.
2. Practice servant leadership.
3. Gather your children.
4. Provide support.
5. Be curious.
6. Catch them being good.

### *1. Show 'em you care through affection and service.*

Just as with our wives, we show mercy to our children through generous affection and cheerful service. Children thrive under the care of affectionate fathers. Studies show that children of affectionate fathers do better on almost every measure of well-being, including academic achievement, moral reasoning, resistance to negative peer influences, and so-called "prosocial" behaviors like thoughtfulness, service, and obedience. There is a saying that goes, "Children who feel good, act good." There is little that helps children feel better than their father's loving care, attention, and approval. Think how much, even at your age, you would give to hear your father say he loves you and that he is proud of who you are, what you have accomplished, or what you are becoming. Some of you reading this know the power of such statements because you have heard your father say such things to you. Other readers know the power of such statements because of their absence. Regardless, all of us can imagine the impact our affection and affirmation can have on our children.

The best gift I ever received was a letter my father wrote to me on my sixteenth birthday telling me how proud he was of the man I was becoming. My parents couldn't afford to give me many of the things my friends got for their sixteenth birthdays, but I wouldn't have traded that letter for the nicest sports car money could buy. If showing mercy means treating others in a manner that reminds them of their worth in God's eyes, it is hard to imagine a more powerful and impactful way to convey this sense of value to our children (those of every age) than by holding them in our arms and telling them we love them, value them, and are proud of who they are and who they are becoming.

In a similar way, doing things for and with our children reminds them they are worth our time and attention. Serving our children doesn't mean waiting on them hand and foot. It means modeling the self-donation, care, and attention we expect them to offer the family in return. A godly father is careful to keep the promises he has made to his children without having to be reminded. He looks for little ways to make their lives easier or more pleasant. He takes interest in their games, projects, and activities. He knows their friends. He takes time to get to know his children's needs and helps them find godly ways to meet them.

### *2. Practice servant leadership.*

Service is critical to commanding godly obedience from our children. St. Ambrose once reflected on the scripture, "You are my friends if you do what I command you" (Jn 15:14). He was confused because friends don't command friends. He realized that Jesus was speaking of a different kind of obedience. Ambrose observed that, while pagans may command one another by force and consequences, insisting upon blind obedience that is enforced by harsh punishments, Christians were called by the Lord's own example to practice a discipleship model of obedience (see Mt 28:19).

How does Jesus "command" us? He loves us (see Jn 13:34). He serves us and meets our needs. We come to see God as the source of everything we are and everything we have. We submit to him, not out of fear of what he is going to do to us if we don't but out of gratitude for his generosity and a sense of expectant hope that, since he has cared for us so well in so many ways, it only makes sense to submit whatever remains of our lives to him. We willingly become his disciples and ask him to teach us the ways that we should go so that we might live more abundantly.

True Christian fathers command obedience in a similar way. Psychologists know from years of solid research (and I have experienced this in my own fathering) that God created children to offer their obedience willingly when fathers take the time to listen to their children's needs and teach them what to do instead of waiting for them to mess up and then punishing them for getting it wrong. Practicing the Spiritual Works of Mercy with our children—in particular, bearing wrongs patiently, forgiving willingly, and admonishing them gently—doesn't mean either letting children off the hook for disobedience or punishing them harshly after the fact. It means taking the time to actively teach them what to do.

I have mentioned before that this is not meant to be a book on parenting techniques. For readers who would like to delve more deeply into effective, Christian approaches to positive discipline, I encourage you to check out *Parenting with Grace: The Catholic Parents' Guide to Raising Almost Perfect Kids*. For our purposes, it is enough to say that, despite much conventional opinion to the contrary, children do not—for the most part—struggle with obedience because they are bad, intentionally stubborn, manipulative, or recalcitrant. In the words of Servant of God Fr. Edward Flanagan, "There are no bad [children]. There is only bad environment, bad training, bad example, bad thinking." Yes, we may have told our children a thousand times that they should do something, and they may be able to write the correct answers on a test of how they should behave, but that's different than knowing how to actually apply what they know in particular situations. It is hard enough for adults to refocus their attention, control their emotions, resist peer pressure, or think on their feet and do the right thing. Imagine how much more difficult it is for a child to master these skills in the heat of the moment. Generally, if our children are struggling to obey us, they do not need punishments. They need help, structure, support, and encouragement. Punishment is like salt in cake batter. More than a pinch is too much. If your children are misbehaving or struggling to follow through on what you have taught them, practice merciful discipline by doing the following.

### *3. Gather your children.*

Because the self-control and attention centers of a child's brain are still developing well into late adolescence, younger children especially can get easily distracted or caught up in the moment. The best way to guarantee that a child will *not* obey you or remember what you told them is to shout a command as you walk through the room on your way to something else.

The things you tell your child to do are important. Your actions should communicate this. The requests you make of your child are important enough to stop what you are doing, bring your child to you, put him on your lap (if he is younger) or at least look him in the eye, tell him what to do, and then ask him to repeat it back to you.

Christian fathers must follow the example of the Good Shepherd. If we want our sheep to follow us, we can't shout at them on our way out the door and then take away their cell phones when they ignore us. We have to gather our little flocks and make sure we have their attention. Yes, it can be a pain. But it is no less than our Lord does for us, and it is much more effective. God created children to resist listening to people who do not take the time to care for them. Knowing this will make you slow down and give your words and your children the attention they are both due.

### *4. Provide support.*

A good shepherd doesn't assume that his sheep will stay put. He assumes that they will naturally wander off if left to their own devices. That's why he provides a nice fence to keep them in a safe space and watches over them to make sure they don't get into a tough spot.

Again, because of the way children's brains develop, you cannot expect most children under eight—and some over—to fulfill more complicated tasks such as getting ready for bed or cleaning their room without some kind of mid-task redirection and accountability. In fact, the more distractions you have in your home—including other children who might interrupt their siblings' tasks—the older a child will have to be before he can be expected to follow through without you checking in and providing ongoing support and guidance. When you ask a child to do something, you need to remain at least within earshot to make sure it is happening; otherwise you should assume it is not being done.

In the Lord's Prayer, we ask God to avoid leading us into temptation. But how often do we set our children up to fail by setting developmentally inappropriate expectations for them, only to swoop in with criticisms and consequences when they inevitably and predictably fail? Don't misunderstand me: children can demonstrate much more responsibility and character than people assume. Most parents don't expect nearly enough from their children in terms of chores, attitude, and the general contribution they can and should be able to make to the well-being of the house and family. But children don't achieve the heights of respectfulness and responsibility without gentle, consistent guidance from a watchful parent. The good shepherd doesn't blame the sheep when they escape the paddock. He recognizes that the fence—and his own attention—were lacking, and he takes steps to address the problem in his system. If good systems are in place, the sheep don't wander from the fold.

### *5. Be curious.*

In the section in this chapter that focused on your relationship with God, we examined the acronym COAL and observed how curiosity, openness, acceptance, and love were the keys to respectful change in yourself. It turns out that COAL is the fuel for creating change in others as well—especially children. When our children misbehave, we must learn to exhibit the same curiosity, openness, acceptance, and love God asks us to give ourselves. When a child doesn't obey, rather than assuming that you have him all figured out and that he was being disobedient for a host of bad and manipulative reasons, you must take the time to be curious and say, "Son (or daughter), I know you know the rules, because we've talked about them often enough. What made it hard for you to do the right thing in that situation?"

When we get the answer, we don't accept excuses, but we are open to what the child has to say. We also accept that learning to be obedient in big things and small things takes time, and so we try to be patient with lapses while making sure to provide the structure and guidance necessary for success. Finally, we love the child, that is, we work for the child's good by teaching him what to do in such situations so that he can succeed the next time. This last step is called "teaching the positive opposite," and it is the key to effective discipline. Your child can't learn to do anything you ask efficiently if you just punish all the wrong options until he figures out the right one. You have to teach him what to do in this particular instance. Talk him through the situation, role-play the right way to do things, create opportunities to practice under your supervision. Train him up by getting on the field and coaching rather than shouting from the sidelines.

### *6. Catch them being good.*

Make sure to tell your children what they do well. Children are eager to please fathers who show that they can be pleased. Catch them being good. Point out good choices. Compliment successes. Note when they control themselves, act generously, behave responsibly, or speak respectfully. Say something about it. You don't have to throw a party or give them a medal for every good deed, but a simple, "That's what I'm talking about. Good job!" will go a long way in helping your child actively work hard to be well-behaved (as opposed to having to drag him to good behavior by scolding and punishing). St. Francis de Sales coined the phrase, "You can catch more flies with honey than with vinegar." This saying applies in spades to effective fathering.

The fifth BeDADitude, "Blessed are the dads who are merciful. They will be shown mercy" doesn't mean letting our children get away with murder. In fact, it means having the same incredibly high standards for them that our heavenly Father has for us. After all, extending mercy means treating people in a manner that reminds them of their worth in the eyes of God, and we are all sons and daughters of the Most High. But it does mean that we must pursue those lofty goals of perfection and divine sonship using only the merciful means our heavenly Father uses with us: loving us, guiding us, and supporting us so that, through his infinite grace, we can become everything we were created to be. The merciful dad combines tremendously high standards with a remarkably gentle touch that lets God's grace flow into the space between himself and his child so that both may be transformed by the loving discipleship relationship that results.

## Questions for Reflection

- How is this merciful approach to fathering similar or different from the way you were raised?
- When do you have the hardest time using COAL to fuel change in your children's behavior? How will you use it to fuel change in this area in the future?

## Prayer

Heavenly Father, help me to be a merciful husband and father. Help me to remind my wife and children of what they are worth in your eyes. Inspire me with your mercy to expect the best from myself, my wife, and my children but to lead with gentle confidence and to support my family's growth with loving guidance. Help me to avoid shouting and criticizing from the sidelines. Give me the grace I need to be an effective coach, teacher, supporter, partner, friend, and shepherd to my family, my flock. Amen.

# THE SIXTH BEDADITUDE

## Blessed are the dads who are pure in heart. They will see God.

To be pure in heart is to be able to see the goodness in both yourself and others. It implies a commitment to never use another person as an object intended for one's own satisfaction. In *Love and Responsibility*, St. John Paul II asserted that the opposite of loving someone is not hating them but using them. Why? If you love someone, you build them up, you help them become more of a person. But if you use them, you tear them down. You treat them less like a person and more like a thing. To be pure in heart means that in all we do, our intentions toward others are good, honest, and ordered toward helping them become fully formed, godly persons—the very best version of themselves.

Jesus says that the pure of heart shall see God. That is a two-fold promise. Of course, it means that those who dedicate their lives to working for the good of others and loving others as God loves them will have a place at the heavenly banquet, but there is a more immediate sense in which this is true as well. Those who are pure in heart are empowered by grace to see God in the face of everyone they encounter. In particular, dads who are pure in heart are given the special gift of seeing God in their wives and children. They are able to marvel at the miraculous gift they have been given, and they dedicate themselves to protecting and nurturing the gift of their family life, carefully guarding the dignity of each person under their care.

## *Blessed Are the Dads Who Are Pure in Heart*

### Your Relationship with God

We cannot give what we do not have. As with all the blessings conveyed by the Beatitudes, being authentically pure in heart begins in your relationship with yourself and God. As I mentioned above, to be pure in heart means having the power to see each individual as a person—not a thing—imbued with godly dignity and worth not because of the function he serves but for the mere fact that he exists and is loved by God. How often do you allow yourself to be seen not as a son of God but as a mere human resource, a tool that is good only to the degree that you can produce something for others—be it money, solutions, or service?

We are told that it is in a man's nature to act, and that is true. In the beginning Adam was created to be a steward of the earth, to till the soil (see Gn 2:5). But doing and acting are only part of our mission. Before we were created to do anything, we were created to be loved. Even while man was still a mere lump of clay, incapable of doing anything, God loved him into being and pronounced him "very good" (Gn 1:31).

Men seem to find it easy to use others. From the way we treat those who work for us to the way we are drawn to pornography and promiscuity, we are constantly tempted to see others as objects—mere means to our material ends. Why? Because many men do not see themselves as more than tools of production. It sounds strange to think of it, but on the most basic level, many—even most—men are not raised to think of themselves as human beings but as human resources, both at work and at home. From childhood, we are praised for the grades we get, the games we win, the way we stack up against others on the playground. As adults, we are valued for the money we make, the projects we accomplish, the things we acquire.

Don't get me wrong. I am not criticizing a healthy male drive for accomplishment and competition. Kept in proper perspective, these pursuits play an important role in fostering a healthy masculine identity. Learning to exercise our abilities, gifts, and strengths is an important part of growing in a sense of ourselves as men, and the *Catechism* teaches that meaningful work is an important way we men assert our dignity as people. But even today we men are raised in a manner that so overemphasizes our need *to do* that we aren't taught to choose "the better part" (Lk 10:42)—that is, to be mindful, to be prayerful, to be empathic, to be relational, to be communicative, and to simply be. Men find it easy to use others because we have come to expect that our worth is entirely tied up in how well we ourselves can be used by others. We dutifully do our part and then are stunned when others resist being treated the way we expect to be treated—as objects who solely exist to get a job done.

Not all men are raised this way, of course. And in fact, our bodies reveal that no man was intended by God to be raised this way. Remember, the theology of the body asserts that we can learn a great deal about who we are and what our destiny is in God by studying how God created our bodies to function. Research in neuroscience reveals what the theology of the body teaches: namely, that men and women differ not in their capacity for mindfulness, prayerfulness, empathy, relationality, communication, or being but in the ways these qualities are expressed through the masculine or feminine body.

For instance, both men and women have been created by God to be fully nurturing—nurturance is an essential quality that all human beings share. But the bodies of men and women have been created in such a way that when they practice their particular brands of nurturance, they stimulate a baby's brain differently. Research shows that the nurturing presence of a mother stimulates the structures of the brain that regulate our fear and stress responses and help babies develop their lifelong biological capacity for stress management. But the presence of a nurturing father stimulates the structures of a toddler's brain that regulate aggression and give the child the ability to control anger and redirect aggressive impulses into productive action. The reason that so many fatherless youths gravitate toward antisocial behavior isn't just social and psychological; it is biological and neurological.

To give these benefits to his child, a father doesn't have to do anything. He just has to be present to his child, be communicative with his child, be empathic with his child, and, in general, be together with his child. In fact, the more a child's father is absent from the home because he is out doing things, the less effective he is at communicating this basic masculine gift to his child's brain. It's not the money the father makes, how often he mows the lawn, or the way he maintains the car that conveys these benefits to the child. It is the mere fact that he is there.

The point I am making is that—in order to be pure of heart as the sixth BeDADitude commands, to rediscover our true, God-given, masculine genius, and, ultimately, to learn to more effectively resist the temptation to use others as objects instead of loving them as persons—we men need to stop seeing ourselves merely in terms of what we can accomplish and instead rediscover our basic humanity. Business guru Stephen Covey made a similar point in his classic book *First Things First* when he illustrated the male tendency to be so consumed by doing what is urgent (paying bills, completing tasks) that men forget to do what is important (reflecting, goal planning, being present to others). Jesus tells us that we are to love others as we love ourselves (see Mk 12:31), but if our capacity to love ourselves as human beings instead of human "doings" is impaired, how can we hope to cultivate the purity of heart that allows us to see others as persons to be loved instead of things to be used? The following represents two ways you can both rediscover and deepen your experience of the masculine gift of being:

1. Reflective prayer.
2. Pursue purity.

### *1. Reflective prayer.*

Men tend to pray in very perfunctory, dutiful ways. We say our prayers. We tell God what we need and, having filled out the appropriate spiritual forms, we get on with the day. Authentic prayer is always a conversation, however. We must do more than talk at God and say words to him. We must listen and respond to what we hear. It is fine to talk to God, but how well do you listen to him? Reflective prayer—cultivating the active ability to hear God speaking to you—is critical to maintaining purity of heart.

Men face a constant battle against the temptation to use others, to treat the people we interact with throughout the day as mere means to our material ends. How can we ever hope to be successful in battle if we can't hear our Commander guiding us through the battlefield, empowering us to achieve our objective—an authentic commitment to work for the betterment of everyone we encounter? In order to achieve this goal, we need to have access to high-level skills such as self-control, sublimation (the ability to channel negative impulses in positive directions), insight (the ability to know what drives us and why), and empathy (the ability to feel how our actions impact others). Research in brain science shows that each of these skills is developed through the practice of mindfulness. Although there are different approaches to mindfulness, for Christians, mindfulness represents the ability to (a) be aware of our impulses and where they come from, (b) be attuned to our environment and the needs of those around us, (c) be engaged in prayerful discernment about the most godly course of action in each moment, and (d) be conscious about the choices we make based upon this discernment. Mindfulness allows these four actions to occur in a split second so that we can cooperate with each moment of grace.

Mindfulness is the science of being. It enables a man to see himself always as a person who has the ability to choose the better part—that is, to see himself and those around him not as objects to be used but as persons who deserve his loving care. The mindful father has discovered that in the space between his impulses and his actions he has a God-given capacity to choose what to do. In every moment, he is either acting in ways that treat others as objects—as things to be used or ignored as he chooses—or he is choosing to practice purity of heart by acting in ways that build up those around him. If he misses the brief window of opportunity (measured in milliseconds) between impulse and action, he runs a high risk of being cut down by the enemy and giving in to ungodly passions, whereby he will allow himself to use or be used by others. If he trains himself well, he will learn to respond rather than react. He will learn to be authentically pure in heart, that is, to be the kind of man who, through God's grace, can consciously choose to act—in every moment—in ways that protect his own dignity and build up everyone around him, reminding them of their worth and potential in God's eyes.

Making this happen requires a high level of awareness that is only possible by maintaining a God's-eye view. Reflective prayer is key to this process. Through reflective prayer, you bring four domains of your experience (your environment; your body; your emotions, thoughts, and memories; and your relationships) into your awareness and place them under God's headship.

In prayer, quiet yourself. Bring each of these four dimensions of your experience to God in turn.

### Your Environment

Ask God to make you aware of what is going on around you. How does the space you are occupying look? What is happening? God is speaking to you through the things that are going on around you. Ask God to make you aware of simple things he is asking you to do to bring more order, grace, or peace to the environment you are in. Are things where they should be? Is something amiss? How might God want you to leave this place better than you found it?

### Your Body

Ask God to make you aware of what is going on inside of you. God made your body and maintains it from moment to moment. Every breath you take is an immediate gift from God. God, being so intimately connected to your existence in this moment, is constantly speaking to you through your body. The tension in your muscles, the feelings in your gut, the tingling of your skin, the rate of your breath and heartbeat—these are all messages from God about how you are responding to this moment. What is God saying to you—through your body—about the choices you are making and about the choices you need to make to be a healthy person, to protect your dignity and integrity, to resist the temptation to use and be used, and, instead, to be authentically pure of heart?

### Your Emotions, Thoughts, and Memories

Many men have learned to ignore their feelings, but your emotions are an incredible source of wisdom, not so much on their own but because they serve as the entry point for discovering the underlying thoughts and memories that guide your actions and choices in every moment. These memories and thoughts serve as the legs on which our emotions stand. Even though many people are not aware of it, every feeling is attended by thoughts and memories that tell us a lot about what we are feeling and why we are feeling it. We spoke about consolations and desolations in the chapter on the third BeDADitude. Remember that consolations are those thoughts, feelings, memories, and impulses that draw us closer to God or the person God wants us to be, while desolations make it harder to do both of these things. Consolations push us toward meaningful, intimate, and virtuous choices—all qualities that facilitate pureness of heart—while desolations lead us to powerlessness, isolation, self-pity, and self-indulgence. Being more aware of our feelings and the thoughts and memories that support them is the key to discerning whether our choices—from moment to moment—are being more informed by the consolations of the Holy Spirit or desolations of the enemy. We cannot be pure of heart if we allow desolations—even unconscious desolations—to rule our emotional lives.

Spend a few minutes each day bringing your feelings to God. They don't have to be big feelings, strong feelings, or even specifically positive or negative feelings. But whatever you are feeling, and to whatever degree you are feeling them, bring these emotions to God. Ask him to make you more aware both of the memories and thoughts associated with those feelings and the degree to which those memories and thoughts are informed by either consolations or desolations. In general, are your emotions leading you closer to or further away from God and the person God wants you to be? Ask God to be the Lord of your emotional life and to help you master your emotions—not by repressing, denying, or minimizing them but by allowing them to be transformed through God's grace into the engines that drive your choices for meaningfulness, intimacy, and virtue in all that you do.

### Your Relationships

We discussed how, in his interior life, God is a communion of persons, a relationship, in the chapter on the second BeDADitude. "Trinity" is the word we use to describe the intimate relationship among Father, Son, and Holy Spirit. Being made in God's image, we too are essentially relational, and God communicates to us through our relationships. It is God's desire that we would be as close to the people who share our lives as grace allows. It was Jesus' personal prayer that all would be one as he and the Father are one (see Jn 17:21).

Take a few minutes a day to bring your relationships—first with your wife and children and second with the important others in your life—to God. As you pray, reflect on the degree of closeness you feel with each person and the degree to which they would say they feel close to you. Are you as close as you would like to be? Have you allowed them to get as close as they would like? Are you giving too much time to certain relationships and not enough to others? What might God want you to do to bring your relationship life into line with his will?

God "speaks" to us in many ways. It is rare that we hear his actual voice, but that doesn't mean he isn't speaking to us continually. He is communicating with us through our environment; through our body; through our emotions, thoughts, and memories; and through our relationships. Praying reflectively about these different areas of our lives enables us to attune more closely to God and act in a manner that is both befitting of our dignity and the dignity of others. By asking God to be the Lord of these four primary domains of our being, we learn to be still and listen to God instructing us—moment by moment—on how to demonstrate true purity of heart, acting in a manner that affirms that both we and those we love are persons to be loved—not things to be used.

## Questions for Reflection

- How do you listen to God currently? How would bringing these four domains of your experience to God enable you to listen to God better?
- How do you think prayerfully reflecting on these four areas of your life on a daily basis would increase your ability to practice purity of heart—that is, your ability to love yourself and others instead of using them?

### *2. Pursue purity.*

Of course, any discussion of purity of heart would be incomplete without discussing the common, fallen, masculine tendency to lust. Lust is not the "sin" of finding a woman attractive—even a woman who is not your wife. In *Love and Responsibility*, St. John Paul II notes that when attraction is pure and united with God's grace, it is simply God's way of calling our attention to another and reminding us to serve them in some way. Attraction is simply God's way of gently pulling us out of ourselves and reminding us that we were created for communion, to come out of our heads and our own concerns and reach out to others in loving service.

Lust, by contrast, turns the godly intention behind attraction inside out. Lust distorts attraction, disables its ability to be used as a force for good, and transforms it into an engine that makes us want to use others. Although we think of lust primarily in terms of a disordered sexual impulse, loosely speaking, we lust anytime we use anyone—male or female—as a means to an end. This is what it means to have a lust for power, a lust for money, or a lust for fame. When I lust, I want something so badly that I will use anything any way I choose to get it.

Being pure of heart means rejecting lust in all its forms. We tend to think of purity of heart in largely negative terms. We think it means not watching certain TV shows or movies or not visiting certain websites or reading certain magazines. Of course it does mean these things, but this is the most superficial understanding of purity of heart. Purity of heart is, ultimately, much more than a commitment to not do certain things (use people). It is a commitment to consciously do other things instead (love them).

Research into problem sexual behavior (that is, sexual addiction) tends to show that men who have a compulsive relationship with pornography and masturbation tend to struggle with true intimacy. They are worse than average at expressing feelings, dealing with interpersonal conflict, or making their needs known to others. They also tend to struggle with being empathic, that is, allowing themselves to feel what others feel and respond in loving and supportive ways to those feelings. In my professional experience, I have found that these descriptors also apply to men who lust for things beyond sex (money, wealth, power, etc.).

Cultivating true purity of heart requires more than putting a filter on your computer. It means challenging yourself to take lustful impulses to use people in any way and heal those impulses at the root. In my book *Broken Gods*, I argue that lust is actually a perversion of the divine longing for communion. We were created for connection, but we settle for stimulation. When you feel an urge to use anyone—be it to indulge in pornography, nurse inappropriate thoughts about a woman you see at the gym, or (for that matter) to use subordinates at the office by making them work in ways that undermine their dignity or are detrimental to their well-being—you must (1) identify the impulse, (2) arrest the impulse, and (3) transform the impulse.

Identifying the impulse probably seems pretty obvious, but because it is so easy to use others, we don't often recognize when we are doing it. You don't need to be scrupulously hard on yourself, but ask God to help you try to become more gently conscious of the times you are tempted to use the people in your life (or allow yourself to be used) in any way. Be aware of this tendency. Write it down when it happens. Work to become better at catching and redirecting yourself before it happens again.

Arresting the impulse to lust doesn't mean condemning yourself or engaging in extreme behavior, such as never being alone with a woman or never turning on the computer unless your wife is in the room. It means that once you observe yourself wanting to use someone, you first stop yourself from going ahead with that impulse and, instead, realize that you are called to do something else. Namely, instead of using the other, you are called to serve and/or create a meaningful connection with this person in some way. Find some way to make this person's (or any person's) life easier or more pleasant. Give an (innocent) compliment, hold the door, turn off the computer and go wash dishes for your wife (or start a conversation with her), or ask your subordinate at work whether he needs any help with a project. Do something that disengages you from the impulse to use another and re-engages in you the action of serving and connecting with another. Ask yourself how you might be kind, thoughtful, loving, and/or appropriately closer to someone in this moment.

Transforming the impulse means that, having identified and arrested the impulse to use someone, next we must transform it by doing the act of loving service we imagined in step two. A funny thing happens if we do this consistently. The former impulse to lust becomes easier and easier to resist. Brain scientists tell us that "neurons that fire together, wire together." They also tell us that when we don't use certain brain pathways, the nerve cells supporting those connections die off. Taken together, what this means is that when we actively use this three-step process for cultivating purity of heart, we are physically taking apart and starving the old lust networks in our brains and creating new networks for godly attraction and loving service. This is hard work—resisting lust takes effort because you are literally rewiring your brain through conscious action—but it is this process that ultimately allows your efforts to cultivate purity of heart, to not merely be something you do but actually become a part of who you are.

## Questions for Reflection

- How does this understanding of lust as the action of using anyone as a means to an end change your understanding of lust?
- When are you most likely to use someone or allow yourself to be used by someone in the course of your day? What could you do to identify, arrest, and transform this moment of lust into a moment of loving service and connection?

To cultivate true purity of heart is to radically commit yourself to routing out any temptation of allowing yourself to be used by others as a means to an end or using others in that manner. We do this by becoming more aware of how God wants us to respond to what is happening around us and inside of us and by reclaiming the godly intention behind attraction—allowing it to motivate us to connect and serve rather than use and throw away.

## Prayer

Father, help me to be truly pure of heart. Help me to become more sensitive to the ways I allow myself to be used as a means to an end and to become more aware of the ways I am tempted to use others in a similar fashion. Help me to identify these impulses to use others, arrest them, and, through your grace, transform them into opportunities to serve others and create the true communion that you created me to seek. Let me be a man who builds up all those I encounter so that I may be an effective instrument of grace in the lives of all who know me.

## *Blessed Are the Dads Who Are Pure in Heart*

### Your Relationship with Your Wife

It is easy to make our wives feel used. Every day I talk to women who say things such as, "I don't know if he thinks I'm good for anything besides cleaning the house, keeping the kids out of his way, and having sex." Such a wife has not been loved as a person in a long, long time.

Even if the situation is not this extreme, it is easy to take one's wife for granted, to simply assume that she is there to make one's life easier. Of course, in a sense she is. In fact, as helpmates, husbands and wives are supposed to make each other's lives easier and more pleasant. But marriage is more than a transaction in which the husband does a, b, and c and expects to be "paid" by the wife doing x, y, and z for him in return. Marriage is a sacrament, an "intimate partnership" (*Gaudium et Spes*) in which the two become one. The process of becoming one, however, is more than a functional partnership in which you scratch her back and she scratches yours. Ultimately, cultivating purity of heart in your marriage means refusing to treat your wife as if she were a vending machine, something that owes you goodies (whether sexual or otherwise) because you pushed the right buttons. Even more importantly, it means committing yourself to cherishing your wife as a person, a helpmate, and the greatest gift God could have ever given you. Let the following ideas be a starting point for practicing purity of heart in your marriage:

1. Cherish your bride.
2. Practice natural family planning.

3. Resist porn—and pornifying your marriage.

## *1. Cherish your bride.*

The opposite of taking your wife for granted is cherishing her. What does it take to make your wife feel cherished?

Research into healthy marriages found that spouses are more likely to feel cherished in their relationship when there is a 20:1 ratio between positive and negative interactions in the couple—and neutral interactions don't count. This number can seem overwhelming at first, but it turns out that "positive interactions" are relatively small things that take less effort than intention. Smiling at your wife, looking in her eyes when she talks to you, giving her a hug, saying "I love you" and "Thank you," listening attentively, holding her hand, giving her a small compliment—these are just a few of the small positive interactions that add up to cherishing your wife. She doesn't need diamonds and big vacations. She just needs you to actively pay attention to her, be kind to her, and find little ways to thank her for being in your life.

I was counseling a couple in which the wife was feeling profoundly taken for granted. Things took a significant turn for the worse when he completely neglected her on her fortieth birthday. She was devastated, and she let him know it. In the individual session I had with him after this serious blunder, we talked about what it would mean for him to start cherishing his wife instead of taking her for granted. He said, "I need to take the focus off of my individual projects and start treating her like she was my most important project." I congratulated him on his insight and agreed that for him especially this would be a remarkable change. This man was a particularly gifted amateur bluegrass musician. He would wake up in the morning thinking about when he could get time to practice, how he could improve his performance, and what new songs he would like to learn. Even on days when he had to work longer hours than he expected, he managed to make time to practice. I asked him to imagine how his marriage would be different if he applied as much energy to cherishing his wife as he did to cherishing his music. He chuckled, first because he knew the attention that he gave to his wife didn't come near what he gave to his music but second because he finally understood the way out of the dark place they had gotten into as a couple. He said, "I think I'd have a whole new wife on my hands."

In our book *For Better FOREVER*, my wife and I offer several exercises that can help husbands and wives do a better job of cherishing each other. One of the simplest techniques is the Love List Exercise. We recommend that spouses write down at least twenty-five simple things that make them feel cherished, appreciated, or cared for. These could be anything from "putting down your phone when I'm talking with you" to "writing me a short love note" to "giving me a hug before you leave for work." The simpler the better. The goal of the exercise is to do at least two easier things for your spouse and one thing that is a bit more of a challenge each day and then spend ten minutes at the end of the day talking about the ways you tried to take care of each other. The conversation piece of the exercise gives couples the opportunity to note the ways they are trying to prioritize each other and to discuss other ways they might be able to be there for each other in the days ahead.

However you decide to approach it, actively and intentionally doing little things throughout the day—every day—to cherish your wife reminds you that she is a person who deserves to be loved instead of an object to be used, disregarded, or taken for granted. Moreover, it reassures your wife that she is your greatest treasure and that she doesn't have to fear that you would ever use her or treat her with neglect. The wife who feels cherished by her husband feels much safer being expressive of her love for you on every level because she never has to doubt that you see her not as an object but as a human being who is worthy of being treated with dignity and love. Her openness to you—emotionally, spiritually, and physically—is a direct sign of the degree to which you are competently expressing purity of heart in your marriage.

## Questions for Reflection

- What does your wife's expressiveness of her love for you say about your efforts to demonstrate purity of heart in your marriage?
- No matter how much a husband cherishes his wife, there is always more he can do to show her that she is his greatest treasure. What are some simple, practical ways you can do more to cherish your wife on a daily basis?

## *2. Practice natural family planning.*

In my own personal experience and in my years of working with couples, I can tell you with absolute certainty that actively learning and practicing natural family planning (NFP) is the best way a husband can practice purity of heart on an ongoing basis in his marriage. When a godly husband actively participates in all the aspects of NFP, especially in continually discussing and praying with his wife about her fertility and what God is communicating to the couple through it, it facilitates purity of heart in the marriage in several different ways.

First, NFP asks the husband to learn to consider the family's overall well-being, and his wife's well-being in particular, over his own physical desire for her. When a couple has discerned that God is asking them to postpone having a child for a time, abstaining isn't always easy. But if you can embrace the challenges that go along with periodic abstinence—if not always perfectly joyfully, then at least willingly, conscientiously, and lovingly—that sends a powerful message to your wife that your desire is truly for her and not just for physical release. The willingness of her man to sacrifice his sexual desire—even if only for a few days a month—for her greater good and the greater good of the family is a powerful testament to a wife that her husband is committed to never even giving the appearance that he wishes to use her, that he always sees her as a person before anything else.

Second, the degree of communication required to do NFP well, and especially lovingly, compels a couple to cultivate a depth of intimacy that other couples would find difficult—if not impossible—to replicate. Why? In part, this is because NFP couples don't have the luxury of skipping out on couple-prayer or intimate conversations like other couples do. They know they need to make the time whether they are tired or busy or not. They have to be intentional and conscientious about managing their fertility together because—unlike other couples—they don't let a pill do their heavy lifting for them.

Sometimes NFP can be particularly challenging for couples. As I said, in those times when a couple has decided that God is asking them to postpone pregnancy, it can be challenging to abstain from sex even for a few days. But in my work with couples, I have found that the worst tensions NFP couples experience occur when the husband acts as if the wife is inflicting NFP upon him. In these situations, the couple may be avoiding the sin of contraception, but that's all. The husband's resentment, childish pouting, and attempts to pressure his wife to engage in illicit sexual activity undermine any emotional, spiritual, or relational benefits of practicing NFP.

But in marriages where the husband takes the lead in using NFP, the story is entirely different. These couples are able to embrace the struggle of periodic abstinence. They are able to pray through it, talk about it, even joke about it together. When the husband isn't just going along with NFP but taking the lead in it, the wife sees that her husband is heroically putting her needs and the greater good of the family above his strongest desires. In my own life I have experienced the blessings of this, and, in the couples I am privileged to work with, I have seen that time and again the husband's leadership in NFP makes his wife love and trust him in a way that other couples can only envy.

There is much confusion over what NFP is and what it entails. I discuss these questions as well as broader questions about Catholic sexuality in my book *Holy Sex! A Catholic Guide to Toe-Curling, Mind-Blowing, Infallible Loving*. Briefly, it is important to understand that NFP is not "Catholic birth control." It is simply information that helps you work with God's design of your wife's body to either achieve pregnancy when you feel God calling you to add another member to your family or avoid pregnancy when you feel God is asking you to take time to strengthen other aspects of your marriage or family life. According to the secular professional journal *Human Reproduction*, NFP is more than 96 percent effective in helping couples avoid pregnancy (more successful than barrier methods in the same study). It is also a first-line treatment for achieving pregnancy among couples experiencing infertility. It can also be used to help your wife monitor her overall reproductive health and catch potential problems much earlier than she would without the information NFP provides. NFP is a powerful tool that, on a practical level, allows you to practice what the Church refers to as "responsible parenthood." Also, with new technology, such as NFP apps featuring complex fertility algorithms and progesterone test strips, NFP is only becoming both more reliable and more user-friendly with time.

When a couple has been called by God to avoid pregnancy for a time, rather than treating the woman's natural fertility like a disease—as contraception does—NFP works by inviting the couple to abstain from intercourse during the few days leading up to ovulation.

In addition to the practical benefits of NFP, there can be remarkable spiritual and relationship benefits as well, some of which I have mentioned above. These benefits do not come from simply recording signs of fertility, but rather from actively praying together and discussing each day—however briefly—what God is saying to you through the information you gain by doing NFP. Is God asking you to have another child? What do you need to do to get ready for this gift? Is God asking you to postpone having another child so that you can take some time to deepen the spiritual or emotional connections within your marriage and family life? What would you need to do to make this happen? Again, addressing all the concerns or questions you might have about the ins and outs of NFP is beyond the scope of this book. To learn more about NFP, contact your diocesan Family Life Office or the Couple to Couple League International at www.CCLI.org.

## Questions for Reflection

- How does the description of NFP above confirm or differ from your understanding of what NFP is, how it is used, and why it is superior to artificial contraception?
- What can you do to take more of an active lead in practicing NFP in your marriage?

### *3. Resist porn—and pornifying your marriage.*

Finally, practicing purity of heart in your marriage means working hard to resist both pornography and the temptation to "pornify" your marriage. Therapists who treat the problems caused by pornography know that the degree to which a man struggles with impurity tends to be directly related to how difficult it is for that man to create heartfelt connections with those around him. This man turns to pornography—and attempts to pornify his marriage by focusing too heavily on kink—because he struggles to appreciate real intimacy.

Secular sex therapist Dr. Linda Hatch addressed this tendency to pornify marriage in an article titled, "Why Isn't Married Sex 'Hot'? And Should It Be?" She wrote,

> Hot sex is the sugar high of sexuality. It is sex that is amped up to a heightened level by some form of fear or other strong emotion. It is not the same as passionate sex. The sexual intensity of a new romantic relationship, the rapture of falling in love, is described in scientific circles as "limerence." This is a biochemically altered state. . . . The preoccupation with hot sex tends to devalue traditional, tame, heterosexual sex as "plain vanilla" sex. Married sex is then seen as needing to dig its way out of old puritanical hang-ups using porn, experimentation, equipment or whatever it takes to make it "hot." . . . This puts pressure on [people] to find ways to make the sex in their relationship equal the hyper-arousal of addictive sexual acting out. If they can't, then they may be left feeling that there is something wrong with them.

Dr. Hatch speaks to the difference I observe in *Holy Sex!* between eroticism (that is, "hot sex") and holy sex (what Dr. Hatch calls "passionate sex"). They are two different realities. Eroticism is sex that is mainly about creating limerence, a chemical high, that pays little attention to real intimacy. Passionate, holy sex, on the other hand, is rooted in the emotional and spiritual intimacy a couple works hard to cultivate all day long by looking for little ways to care for one another, attend to each other, and celebrate their partnership. The couple that has mastered the art of holy sex understands that sex is a language that speaks not to their ability to turn each other into amateur porn stars but to their incredible partnership that says, "Look how well we work for each other's good all day long! Even our bodies are learning to work for each other's good."

Celebrating holy sex does not mean that a couple can't be playful or spontaneous, experiment with different sexual positions, wear lingerie, or do any other moral activity they might enjoy. It just means that these things aren't the point of their relationship. Intimacy is. Respect is. Love is.

A wife whose husband is focused on eroticism or "hot sex" often feels that she has to protect herself from her lover. And even if she enjoys the sensations of their encounter, she often feels used and ashamed afterward. By contrast, the husband who takes the lead in celebrating holy sex—a passionate, playful, loving sexuality rooted in partnership, prayer, and intimacy—will enable his wife to fulfill her true sexual potential, freeing her to be a generous, passionate lover, without fear of being used or ashamed.

Likewise, when the husband who focuses on eroticism experiences untimely or inappropriate sexual urges, he simply indulges them through pornography, masturbation, or pressuring his wife for satisfaction. By contrast, the husband committed to creating marital intimacy rooted in holy sex channels these same untimely or inappropriate urges into healthy expressions of love: looking for opportunities to serve his wife or otherwise draw closer to her through prayer, communication, or planning fun dates where they can share new experiences and learn more about each other. It isn't always easy to do this, but it is worth it, and both the husband and wife benefit in deep and profound ways from the effort this sacrifice requires.

## Questions for Reflection

- How does the vision of sexuality presented here challenge your vision of sexuality and sexual love?

- In what ways might eroticism tend to negatively impact both your own sexual behavior in and outside of your marital relationship?
- How would practicing holy sex in your marriage change the dynamic between you and your wife?

### Prayer

Heavenly Father, help me to cherish my wife, to never see her as an object to be used for my satisfaction but as a person—my friend and partner—who deserves to be loved and treasured by me as you love and treasure her. Give me the generosity of spirit, self-control, and courage to love her as you would have me love her, so that I might melt her defenses and enable her to see me as a man after your own heart. Amen.

## *Blessed Are the Dads Who Are Pure in Heart*

### Your Relationship with Your Children

In the chapter on hungering and thirsting for righteousness, we discussed the critical role fathers play in the formation of godly children. Recall the finding that children raised in a home where the father does not take the lead in the faith and moral formation of his children have about a 4 percent chance of continuing in the values they were raised in. Your moral example and leadership in your home are critical to your children's ability to be godly, moral men and women.

Encouraging your children to exhibit purity of heart involves more than simply teaching them "the rules" and telling them to save sex for marriage. Certainly, it begins there, but beyond this, it means modeling authentic love in your relationship with them so they can identify real love when they experience it, forming them as whole persons and enabling them to choose to love others rather than use them. Let's look at each of these components to raising purehearted children:

1. Give them moral instruction.
2. Model authentic love.
3. Form them as whole persons.
4. Teach them to choose love over use.

### *1. Give them moral instruction.*

Although it cannot end here, raising well-formed, moral children begins with teaching them the truth about their sexuality and about sexual morality. In *Beyond the Birds and the Bees: Raising Sexually Whole and Holy Kids*, my wife and I note that morality is not about rules; it is about cultivating the ability to love and work for the good of everyone we encounter—including ourselves.

A rule-based morality is severely limited. It makes a great deal of difference to my wife whether I am faithful to her because I "have" to be or if I am faithful to her because I love her. In the same way, the child who simply follows the rules may be pharisaically doing the right thing, but the child who does the right thing as a matter of course—because it is the loving way to treat another person—is a godly child, a child who is truly pure of heart.

It is our job as godly fathers to raise children who not only know and follow the rules but understand that the rules exist not to make us miserable, complicate our lives, or give us a way to appease an angry, prudish God but to help us decide what it means to be loving people and to treat others in loving ways.

To that end, when we have discussions about morality (sexual or otherwise) with our children, we cannot simply tell them, "Don't do that or else." We have to explain why doing the moral thing is the equivalent of doing the loving thing. Early on, teach your children that when they say, "I love you," and when you say, "I love you," to them, you are exchanging a promise. What you are really saying when you tell someone you love them is, "I promise to always build you up, to look for ways to make your life better, and to help you be the person God wants you to be." Saying "I love you" doesn't always mean "I have warm, fuzzy feelings for you," but it does always mean "I will never treat you as anything less than the treasure you are."

When it comes to communicating moral truths about our children's sexuality, the *Catechism* reminds us that God gave us our sexuality so that we could share everything we are—our past, present, and future selves—with another person. Popularly, people often speak of "body language." Our gestures, posture, and facial expressions all "say" something to others. Making love with someone "says," "I give my whole self to you—everything I am and I ever will be. I promise to use my whole self to work for the good of your whole self for the rest of my life."

It is true that many people don't know or believe that sex communicates a promise, but this does not change the reality of things. Our bodies respond to sex as if a lifetime promise has been made. Brain science shows that when two people have sex, their brains begin to think of the other person as part of their own bodies. In fact, when we break up with someone, brain imaging shows that the same parts of our brain light up as when we experience a broken arm or broken leg. We know that repeatedly making and breaking sexual bonds with multiple partners does damage to the structures of the social brain that make permanent bonding with a lifelong partner more difficult. To love someone else, and to truly love ourselves, we save sex for marriage—not because crusty old men in silly, pointy hats told us God would be mad if we didn't but because working for our good and the good of others means promising to never do anything that would hurt them. Having recreational sex with others hurts them—whether they realize or not—not just on a spiritual and emotional level but on a biological, neurological level. We cannot be moral people—that is, truly loving people—unless we at least avoid hurting the people we claim to care about.

## Questions for Reflection

- How do the ideas about morality and sexuality presented here differ from your own moral and sexual formation?
- What difference would applying these ideas make to your current efforts to raise children who are pure in heart?

## *2. Model authentic love.*

In order to raise children who are pure in heart, they have to be able to recognize real love when they see it.

The first way we can do this is to actively take the lead in creating as loving a marriage as we can with our wives. It is not for nothing that past University of Notre Dame president Fr. Theodore Hesburgh is thought to have said, "The best thing a father can do for his children is to love their mother." If we want our children to save themselves for marriage, we have to take the lead in presenting a vision of marriage that is worth saving themselves for. If the love we give to our wives doesn't seem to our children to be more authentic, more genuine, more affirming, more true than the facsimiles of love they encounter in the world, then we have lost the war before the battle has even begun. Research consistently shows that children are more likely to own the values of their youth when they experienced those values as the source of the warmth in their home growing up. The ways you attend to, affirm, and cherish your wife in your day to day relationship give you the credibility you need to effectively disciple your children toward a godly way of life.

Second, be affectionate with your children. Build them up. Affirm them. Hug them. Make time for them. Play their games. Be actively interested in their lives. Don't just say "I love you" and then trust they'll figure it out because you work hard all day. Show them what real love looks like in your one-on-one interactions with them, so that when they are looking for someone to date, they can intuitively choose well. The affection, affirmation, and presence you give to your boys and girls teaches them what to expect from a relationship. It teaches your children—again, both boys and girls—how to treat a spouse and how to expect to be treated by a spouse.

It doesn't matter if affection comes naturally to you or not. Neuroimaging studies show that affection actually helps to beef up the wiring in the moral brain so that the different parts of the brain that can experience an impulse, evaluate the relational consequences of that impulse, and then channel that impulse in healthy directions can communicate with each other more efficiently and more rapidly. It may sound surprising to some, but we now know that the more affection children are given, the more their social brains develop the ability to not only know what to do but to be able to choose to do the right thing in the moment, under pressure, when self-control and higher-level thinking are hardest. Being affectionate with your children doesn't just benefit them emotionally, it supports and fosters the neurological infrastructure that helps them make good moral choices.

## Questions for Reflection

- What messages do your children get from the way you love your wife? What more could you do to give your children an example of a marriage worth saving themselves for?

- How do you show affection to your children? What more could you do to demonstrate your love, pride, and concern for them so that they have the formation they need to recognize real love when they encounter it and choose to be authentically loving people in their interactions with others?

### *3. Form them as whole persons.*

In *Beyond the Birds and the Bees*, my wife and I note that "chastity" is not a single virtue. Rather, it is interaction of eight different virtues: namely, self-donative love, faith (that is, personal connection to God), responsibility, respect, intimacy (that is, emotional/verbal communication), collaboration, joy, and personhood (that is, a healthy respect for both one's body and respective masculinity/femininity). The degree to which a child is well-formed in each of these virtues is the degree to which your child will find it both desirable and easier to remain chaste.

It is beyond the scope of this book to discuss in depth how these qualities facilitate chastity, but as the *Catechism* notes, chastity refers to the effective integration of sexuality within the whole person. That's a complicated way of saying that being chaste doesn't simply mean that we know how to keep our pants zipped up. It means that we know how to take pleasure in loving every person as fully as we can, in the best way we can, depending upon the context we are in.

The person who is chaste will truly enjoy lovemaking with his or her spouse, but he or she will also really enjoy talking, sharing, praying, serving, and participating in nonsexual affection. The person who is truly chaste does not experience these activities as a poor substitute for sex. He or she understands them as the best way to be loving to a particular person in the particular context he or she is in. He or she finds the experience enjoyable for what it is and does not try to force it to be something it is not so that it can "really count" as connection with the other.

Obviously this takes more than just knowing "da rulz." It requires being a fully formed person who knows how to share himself or herself appropriately with others. Of course, all of us struggle to be perfectly chaste. Because chastity involves the complete and healthy integration of sexuality within our personhood, true chastity is a lifelong project. But the degree to which a person struggles to be chaste will be directly rooted in deficits in one of the eight qualities we identified above. Raising a child who is pure of heart means doing everything you can to foster the eight virtues that make your child a *mensch* (a Yiddish word for an "all-around, deep down good person"). To know how likely it is that your child will have the integration necessary to be chaste—not just until marriage but beyond (because healthy marriages still require good sexual stewardship)—reflect on each of your children's capacities for living out each of the eight qualities I identified above. Work on fostering any of the qualities you feel a particular child may need to shore up. This is the true work of forming your children in chastity: helping them become the whole persons they need to be to determine for themselves the best way to be loving to each person they encounter based upon the context in which they find themselves.

## Questions for Reflection

- How does this understanding of chastity (as a construct of eight virtues that facilitate the healthy and proper expression of love dependent upon the person and context) differ from your previous understanding of this concept?
- Reflect for a moment on each of your children. In which of the eight qualities identified in the chapter (self-donative love, faith, responsibility, respect, intimacy, collaboration, joy, and

personhood) is each child strongest? Which qualities might each child need your help to develop?

### *4. Teach them to choose love over use.*

Finally, take whatever opportunities you have to highlight the difference between loving and using someone. Look for examples that occur in the shows your children watch, the stories they tell about their friends at school, or even the choices they make in dealing with friends, brothers and sisters, and you and your wife. If you see your children treating other people as means to an end, quietly ask them if they are making a "loving choice" or a "using choice." Help your children notice the little temptations we all encounter to use people rather than build them up and treat them with dignity. Laying this groundwork in little ways will help your children be more sensitive to using and being used by others as they become young adults.

Taking these steps can help you begin to shepherd your children down the path toward greater purity of heart as adults.

Jesus promises that those who are pure in heart will see God. By cultivating purity of heart in yourself and in your home, you will not only be given the grace to see God in the next life but you will also be empowered to see God in the face of your spouse, your children, and every person you meet. And those who encounter you will see the loving face of God shining out through your eyes.

## Questions for Reflection

- In what little ways do you see your children using others? How could you gently raise your children's awareness of the call to choose love over the temptation to use others?

## Prayer

Heavenly Father, help me to model a pure heart for my children and teach them to exhibit purity of heart in all their dealings with others. Give my children the wisdom to see the difference between using and loving others and to only choose to be in relationships with those who would love them. Help me and each person in my family to see you. Amen.

# THE SEVENTH BEDADITUDE

## Blessed are the dads who are peacemakers. They will be called children of God.

For fathers, being peacemakers involves more than stopping the kids from destroying the house and setting the dog on fire. It means creating a strong, secure homelife. St. Augustine wrote, "Peace is the tranquility that results from right order."

We often think that being peacemakers means avoiding conflict and "not sweating the small stuff." While it is certainly important to pick our battles, it is often too easy to fall into the trap of mistaking mere quiet for authentic peace. As I note in *Broken Gods: Hope, Healing, and the Seven Longings of the Human Heart,* quiet is Satan's plagiarism of peace. Quiet tells us that the best way to achieve peace is to ignore real problems that are happening right in front of us, to check out, to consciously choose to ignore the disorder in our lives, marriages, or families because "I just need a break." This kind of "peacemaking" is actually the deadly sin of sloth, which is not laziness so much as it is a stubborn refusal to care.

True peacemaking, on the other hand, requires us to be actively engaged in the process of setting things right in our lives. Being peacemakers means committing to creating godly order in our lives and relationships so that God's peace can reign in our hearts and in our homes.

## ***Blessed Are the Dads Who Are Peacemakers***

### Your Relationship with God

Inner peace often escapes us. St. Augustine once said, "What good is peace in the world if we are at war with ourselves?" While there are many things that cause us to experience inner conflict, one of the biggest contributors is our inability to achieve an appropriate work-life balance.

While meaningful work is an important source of human dignity and self-esteem, 1 Peter 3:7 reminds us husbands of the importance of prioritizing our marriages and family lives, "so that [our] prayers may not be hindered." God wants us to give the best of ourselves—not just what's left of ourselves—to our spouses and children.

Many men intuit this, but they get so much validation from their work that it's hard to give up the addiction to praise and accomplishment. Psychiatrist Thomas Szasz once wryly noted, "How men hate waiting while their wives shop for clothes and trinkets; how women hate waiting, often for much of their lives, while their husbands shop for fame and glory."[4]

Instead of admitting and embracing our innate, God-given need for connection, intimacy, and communion—in particular with our wives and children—we get angry at our families for being "needy" or "demanding" or "not appreciating how hard we work." Of course they appreciate how hard we work. They just appreciate *us* more and wish we could find it in our hearts to "choose the better part," to stop running around from project to project and simply be with them. How sad it is that so many men have been raised in a manner that makes them think that someone loving them enough to be desperate to spend time with them is a bad thing. And of course it tears us apart.

The key to being peacemakers—that is, seeking the "tranquility that results from right order"—in our relationships with ourselves is getting our priorities in order and seeking a healthy work-life balance. Where do we start?

In *God Help Me! This Stress Is Driving Me Crazy,* I offer a comprehensive priorities exercise that I have found to be useful in bringing order to my own busy life and helping my clients satisfy their work commitments while making time for their families and assessing how much time they may have left for other pursuits (hobbies, friends, other interests).

I will not present the entire exercise here, but the first step will at least give you a sense of how you might need to reorder your priorities to begin to create the inner peace that comes from giving your family the time it is due. Think of a week when you, your wife, and your children got along better than usual. Don't pick a vacation week. Choose a regular week in which all of you got along—if not completely perfectly, at least better than you usually do. Ask yourself, "How many hours did we spend doing things together in that week? How many meals did we have together? When did we work together? pray together? play together? How much time did we spend talking with each other or, as Pope Francis likes to put it, 'wasting time with each other'?" If you get stuck, talk it over with your wife and kids. Come up with at least a ballpark figure that lets you know the number of hours you spend together when you are at your best as a couple and as a family. This number represents the objective number of hours your family needs to function well. It represents your Family-Time Economy.

Just as cars run on gas, relationships run on time. Likewise, just as different cars have different rates of fuel economy, different relationships have different rates of time economy. It doesn't pay to complain about the amount of fuel your car uses. You bought the car you have, and you've got to give it fuel if you want to make it go. The same thing is true with your marriage and family life. Your family takes the time it takes to make it work. You made it. You need to feed it (or accept responsibility for choosing to starve it).

The number of hours that represents your Family-Time Economy is, again, the minimum number of hours your family needs each week to function well. This is the number of hours you need to carve out for your family each week *if* you want to be able to enjoy the joy, peace, connection, and love God intends you to get out of your family.

Perhaps you are not in a place to be able to give your family this much time each week. That's OK—for now. But the gap that exists between the time you can give your family and the time your family needs to function well represents the chasm you will have to work to fill—over the course of time—in order to experience "the tranquility that results from right order" in your own heart regarding how you spend your time and energy.

## Questions for Reflection

- In light of the priorities exercise described above, how does the amount of time you currently spend with your family compare to the amount of time your family actually needs to function well?
- What would need to change in your life to begin giving your family the time that it needs to function well?
- What small steps could you begin to take this week to begin to create the peace in your heart that comes from giving the amount of time and energy God is asking you to give to your wife and children?

## Prayer

Heavenly Father, you make time out of the busiest schedule in the universe to be imminently present to your Bride, the Church, and to all of your children. Help me to find the peace that comes from knowing I am giving my wife and children the best of myself, my time, and my energy. Help me to be faithful to all of my responsibilities but in a way that helps me remember to choose the better part and be genuinely present in my marriage and family life. And just as your children find peace in your presence, help my presence be a source of peace in my family. Amen.

## *Blessed Are the Dads Who Are Peacemakers*

### Your Relationship with Your Wife

Consciously making time to spend with your wife and children is the first step to being a peacemaker in your home, but in order to experience peace in your marriage and family life you need to spend that time in a "rightly ordered" way that actually leads to fruitful peace. Making more time for your marriage and family just so you can all stare at separate screens in the same room or wander around the house engaging in individual pursuits misses the point and will not lead to peace.

In order to have a peaceful marriage, a couple must commit to rituals that give them the time they need to work, play, talk, and pray together. More than sixty years of research on the power of rituals all but proves that the more committed a couple is to regular working, playing, talking, and praying rituals, the stronger the marriage is and the happier the couple will be.

Rituals of connection facilitate peace in your marriage by giving you the opportunity to create shared experiences that help you understand where each other is coming from, assume a positive intention behind each other's actions, really know how to work together in different contexts, get each other's inside jokes, complete each other's sentences, and create the kind of peaceful tranquility that comes from a rightly ordered connection.

Furthermore, in my work with couples I often find that a tremendous source of marital strife is the feeling wives have that they are forced to beg their husbands to make time for one or more of these four categories of rituals. By contrast, when husbands take the lead in lovingly carving out regular daily and weekly times to work, play, talk, and pray with their wives, their wives are much more understanding and supportive when unexpected work or other crises come up and their husbands need to be away. Knowing that she is loved and desired, and that you always do your best to give her the best of yourself, gives her the room to be as generous as you would like her to be.

As I hinted earlier, couples need at least ten to fifteen minutes per day and at least an hour or more per week to connect across each of these four relationship dimensions. Couples can be creative about this. For instance, a couple might use a work ritual to also get some more important talking time in. You should feel free to do this in a way that works for you. That said, the point is that it is important for you to take the lead in attending to all the different dimensions of a healthy relationship.

Daily work rituals include things like doing the dishes, picking up the family room after the kids have gone to bed, bathing the children and getting them ready for bed, and so on. Weekly work rituals usually mean making some time to make progress on various household projects together. Working together builds trust by helping you know you can count on your partner to show up and help out. It builds gratitude because it helps you feel good about having a partner to help you maintain the life you are building together. It builds closeness and intimacy by helping you learn from each other and be true helpmates to each other.

Daily play rituals involve simple things you enjoy doing together: taking a walk, playing a few hands of cards or a video game you both enjoy, or just being silly together. Weekly play rituals usually involve some kind of a date night (in or out of the house depending on the age of your kids). Playing together enables you to laugh with each other, share new experiences, and remind each other why you are working so hard.

Daily talk rituals involve making time each day for conversations on topics other than which kid needs to be taken where and what needs to be gotten at the store. Taking even fifteen minutes to talk about how close or distant you feel toward each other (and, if the latter, what to do about it), your hopes and dreams, what you might need from each other, or what makes your day a little easier or more pleasant can make all the difference in the world. Weekly talk rituals take these and similar topics to a deeper level.

Some men don't consider themselves "talkers" or "deep thinkers." You don't have to be Abraham Lincoln to have meaningful conversations with your wife. The good news is that psychology proves that, with practice, every man can get better at communicating his thoughts and feelings. In fact, it's good for your mental health. Brain research shows that keeping thoughts and feelings inside causes your right brain to work too hard ruminating about problems rather than solving them. Even when you think you're just "moving on" or "letting it go," unless you've talked it out, your right brain is still churning away, creating emotional and physical stress just under the surface. When you talk out your thoughts and feelings, it activates your left brain, whose job is to critically listen to what's being said, evaluate what's true and what's false, and make a plan to do something about all those feelings the right brain creates. Talking things out with your wife might feel like a chore, but it's a chore worth getting good at, because men who resist these kinds of conversations run a very high risk of depression, alcoholism, infidelity, high blood pressure, inflammatory diseases, and other serious mental, relational, or physical problems. According to Harvard Medical School, lacking the strong emotional connection that good marital communication facilitates increases your risk of premature death by 50 percent and is more dangerous to your health than smoking fifteen cigarettes a day, being overweight, and/or never exercising. Yes, it might be hard. At first it might even feel like work. Don't worry. You *can* do this. *Make. It. Happen.*

Because it doesn't require physical effort, don't be afraid to combine your talk time with other rituals. In fact, having something else to concentrate on, like the dishes or a walk, can make it easier to have more intense conversations. Having something else to focus on can give you time to think out what you want to say and avoid reacting to every little expression or gesture. However you do it, just remember how valuable talking about feelings, future hopes and dreams, struggles, and emotional/spiritual needs is to both relational and personal health. Make regular time for it each day and each week.

We've discussed the importance of couple prayer and marital prayer rituals several times throughout the book. I won't belabor the topic now except to say that creating daily and weekly prayer rituals means making specific appointments to pray. Don't just hope it will happen. Make time for it.

Taking the lead in creating and maintaining time to work, play, talk, and pray together on a regular basis empowers you to be a peacemaker in your marriage by establishing the right order that makes tranquility possible. It helps you give the best of yourself to your wife and enables you to show her that your marriage is—as it should be—your most important commitment.

## Questions for Reflection

- What work, play, talk, or prayer rituals do you and your wife already have? If you were to make more of a commitment to these rituals of connection, where would you start and what would you do?
- What difference do you think it would make in your marriage to take the lead in initiating regular daily times (however brief)

to work, play, talk, and pray together? Do you think it would lead to a more peaceful relationship with your wife?

- How do you think your life would be better if you could take the lead in making regular time to work, play, talk, and pray with your wife?

### Prayer

Heavenly Father, every day you make time for your Bride, the Church; you work alongside her to build your kingdom; you give her reasons to smile and rejoice by blessing her; you share your heart and your will with her; and you lead her into deeper communion with yourself. Help me to be inspired by your example to take the lead in making time to work, play, talk, and pray with my wife, that I might work to create a more peaceful marriage in which you might be glorified. Amen.

## *Blessed Are the Dads Who Are Peacemakers*

### Your Relationship with Your Children

If rituals of connection are important for a peaceful marriage, daily and weekly appointments to work, play, talk, and pray together are critical for a peaceful family life.

Family life is an activity, not an accessory. Many fathers today tend to think of "family life" as the thing that automatically happens in the few minutes a day when everyone is under the same roof (whether or not everyone is actually interacting with one another). Frankly, this is as absurd as thinking that a football game is the thing that spontaneously happens when the people that belong to both teams just happen to be walking through the stadium at the same time on their way to another important meeting. If a team isn't meeting every day to practice, to drill, and to learn to work, think, and play together, it isn't a team. At best, it's a mob. In exactly the same way, if you, as a father, are not insisting that your family make regular daily and weekly appointments to work, play, talk, and pray together, then you don't have a family. At best you have a group of people who live under the same roof and share a data plan.

Being a peacemaker in your home means creating the right order that allows tranquility to exist. This necessarily requires you to be willing to set limits on the kinds of activities your kids may be involved in outside the family. In today's world, this can seem heretical, if not downright antisocial. A few short decades ago, it was assumed that family life was the place where children learned the most important lessons about socialization, values, and how the world worked. In that not-so-distant but now long-forgotten era, children were allowed to participate in extracurricular activities only to the degree that these activities did not interfere with things like family meals, family church attendance, and other important family commitments. The world has changed.

Today, we live in the third generation of the culture of divorce, a world in which 55 percent of children do not live in households with both their mother and father. Even intact families have bought into the idea that it is the community's job, not the family's responsibility, to socialize children. Today, it is considered normal—even desirable—for children to be so over scheduled that they barely see their family, much less have time to work, play, talk, or pray with them. A recent study found that the average parent spends thirty-four minutes a day with their children and a total of ninety-seven minutes together on weekends. Worse, even when families are together, 60 percent of parents report that they spend that time watching TV or using digital devices.

A peaceful family life is predicated upon having children who know, listen to, and follow their parents. It is impossible to feel tranquil in your home if you are living with a bunch of people who don't understand each other, don't listen to each other, and are constantly off doing their own thing. Creating this discipleship dynamic, where your children know, listen to, and follow you, requires laying aside time to cultivate it. Being a father who is a peacemaker in his home means being a father who insists that family life must be the activity that comes first. Period. No exceptions.

That said, you cannot simply say no to activities that conflict with family life and then not plan an actual family life. It would be absurd to tell your children they could not participate in some extracurricular activities just so they can sit at home and watch you stare at your smartphone. Just like a team has practices, meetings, fundraisers, and other activities as well as games, families must intentionally meet around regularly planned appointments to work, play, talk, and pray together. When you make these regular daily and weekly commitments, your children get to know you. They learn your expectations, your likes and dislikes, what you value and believe, and how to please you. They learn to listen to your instructions, advice, and counsel on how to complete tasks, solve problems, and rise to life's challenges. And they learn to follow you as you disciple them in becoming the young men and women of God they are called to be.

In family life, peace is predicated upon parents having a discipleship relationship with their children (that is, one in which children know, listen to, and follow them). Research consistently shows that the degree of influence you have on your children is predicted by the amount of time you spend interacting with them. Your children will know, listen to, and follow (that is, become disciples of) the people with whom they spend the greatest amount of their time. Those people need to be you and your wife. If you choose to let it not be you—by not taking advantage of whatever opportunities you have to create rituals of connection where you and your children regularly work, play, talk, and pray together—then you are, in effect, saying to your children, "Don't listen to me. Go listen to those other people I let you spend all your time with." If you don't want those people (peers and neighbors) forming your kids, don't let your kids spend the majority of their time with everyone but you. It truly is as simple as that. So many parents are terrified of "the media," peer influence, "the culture," and many other modern-day bogeymen. I don't meant to entirely dismiss these concerns. There are real dangers associated with each of these influences.

But the real problem is that parents are worrying about things they have no control over. You cannot control what television programs, movies, or songs are produced. You cannot save the Internet all by your lonesome. You have absolutely no say over the moral life of your children's friends. But you do have absolute control over whether or not you establish the rituals of connection in your household that give you the time you need with your kids to be the most powerful influence in their lives, thereby all but eliminating the negative potential these other influences have on your children. This might strike you as a remarkable claim, but I can tell you I have seen this reality played out in my own children's lives as well as in the lives of friends and clients who follow these principles.

If you establish strong rituals of connection in your family life, your children can fully participate in the culture, have a wide variety of friends, engage diverse points of view, and even encounter evil in the world and still remain largely resistant to it. The vast, half-century-deep body of research on the power of rituals to make kids largely resistant to whatever negative influences the world can throw at them backs up these claims.

By investing the time and energy it takes to create solid rituals of connection that give you regular daily and weekly times for you to work, play, talk, and pray with your kids, you will be a peacemaker several times over. You will give your kids the peace that comes from having a solid base to call home and an available, committed mentor (you) to turn to for guidance and support. You will give your wife peace by letting her see that she can count on you to know what is truly important and stand up for her and her children in the face of a world that wants to tear your family away from you. You will experience the peace in your own heart that comes from living your life in right order and enjoying the tranquility that results from placing your vocation to your family first.

Jesus promises that fathers who are peacemakers will be called sons of God. By making peace, you participate in God's offer of divine sonship by establishing the right order that allows God's grace to flow more freely in your home and in the world. Choosing to create a peaceful home life that is committed to putting first things first makes a bold assertion to the world that, while others may choose to pursue earthly distractions, you and your house will serve the Lord (see Jos 24:15).

## Questions for Reflection

- As a child, to what degree did your family of origin have established rituals for working, playing, talking, and praying together? How do you think the presence (or absence) of these rituals affected you growing up?
- As a child, with whom (or with what) did you spend the most time? How did these people (or activities) impact you growing up?
- With whom (or what) do your children spend the most time interacting? How do you see those influences playing out in their lives? Do you see those influences supporting or distracting from your ability to raise godly children?
- What rituals regarding work, play, talk, and prayer do you already have in your daily life as a family? What ways does your family gather weekly to work, play, talk, or pray together?
- If you were going to create stronger rituals of connection, in which of the four areas (work, play, talk, or prayer) would it be easiest to start?

## Prayer

Heavenly Father, you make time out of the busiest schedule in the universe to connect with us as your children and incline our hearts to yourself. Help me to invest in my family and to turn my children's hearts to you through the connection I facilitate in my home. Help me be an instrument of peace in my family so that we all might enjoy the gift of family life and the tranquility that flows from a rightly ordered household. Amen.

# THE EIGHTH BEDADITUDE

## Blessed are the dads who are persecuted for the sake of righteousness. Theirs is the kingdom of heaven.

Being a father isn't easy. And, as you know by now, being a father who is committed to living the Beatitudes in his fatherhood comes with special challenges. But in the face of those challenges, Jesus offers a word of encouragement, reminding all those who are persecuted for the sake of righteousness that the kingdom of heaven is theirs.

The persecution we encounter can come from surprising places. Sometimes it comes from within ourselves, when we wonder whether the sacrifices we make to put our wives and children before ourselves are really worth it. Sometimes the persecution comes from outside our homes, when employers, extended family, or others get angry that we are not putting them above our vocation to marriage and family life. Most painful of all, sometimes the persecution comes from inside our very own homes, such as when our wives do not share our faith or values or when our children rebel against the love we want to give them and the lessons we wish to convey.

Wherever and however we experience persecution for prioritizing our faith and family lives, we can take comfort in the fact that God finds these sacrifices worthy of praise, that, in fact, more than almost anything else, these sacrifices conform us to Christ, who gave up everything so that his children could come home to him.

## *Blessed Are the Dads Who Are Persecuted*

### Your Relationship with God

We live at a time when there are more competing demands placed on our time than ever. Digital devices increase our productivity, but they also mean that many of us are never truly able to leave work behind. There is a constant fear that if we don't attend to the latest work crisis that pops up in our inboxes right now that we will be judged to be underperforming and uncommitted to the job. We obsessively check our e-mail and watch the latest project updates in Dropbox or Google Docs while going through the motions of attending our kids' games or recitals. Family is seen as a hindrance in most workplaces, and allowances for family life are grudgingly given, if at all.

Employers aren't the only people that fathers find it difficult to disappoint. I regularly talk with men in counseling who find it painfully difficult to say no to anyone other than their own wives and children. They are terrified to set limits with their bosses, parents, friends, pastors, or others who might be disappointed by their unavailability due to their need to put family first.

Sometimes the feared potential fallout from these situations is very real. I have had clients whose employers have told them outright that they need to make peace with the fact that "everyone in the office is on their second or third marriage." In such corporate cultures, employees wear their divorce decrees like badges of honor that testify to what it takes to "make it" in their chosen fields.

Likewise, I have known men whose parents have refused to speak to them because they needed to say no to a request to come to a particular birthday party or other extended family event because they needed to spend time with their own families. Being on the receiving end of these kinds of messages can be painful and demoralizing. In the face of such pressures, it takes an extra measure of grace to stay faithful to our godly priorities of faith and family and avoid falling prey to the false gods of achievement and approval seeking. But we need to recall the importance of choosing well and serving the Lord at all times. As Jesus put it, "What profit is there for one to gain the whole world and forfeit his life?" (Mk 8:36).

Just as often—if not more so—the persecution comes from within. Even when employers, parents, and important others would be completely understanding of our need to put our faith and families first, we torment ourselves with the idea that we won't measure up, will be found wanting, or will, somehow, be thought of as "less than" if we follow through on our commitments to be truly present on the home front. If we aren't careful in our attempts to silence these desolations, we end up neglecting our wives and children while telling ourselves that we have no choice but to jump through the hoops the world puts in front of us—whether real or imagined.

But Jesus tells us that the truth will set us free (see Jn 8:32), and the truth is that you are not anyone's trained monkey. You are a son of God (see 2 Cor 6:18). To paraphrase St. John Vianney, the only public we need to try to please is our heavenly Father and his angels. This is more than pious sloganeering. Our sense of who we belong to dictates how we respond to others. Whether you see yourself as a man of God, a company man, or a mama's boy makes a big difference in how you relate to your priorities. The company man can't say no to his boss. The mama's boy can't set limits with his family of origin. Ironically, only the man who belongs to God can experience the freedom he needs to be his own person. A boss or a parent may want us to live for them, but God is glorified when his creation achieves its destiny, and so only men of God can find the freedom from the fear of persecution to be their true selves.

And what does it mean to be free to be our true selves? Our faith teaches that fathers find themselves by making a free and total gift of themselves primarily to their wives and children. Why? Because marriage is our vocation. A vocation is the primary way a Christian is called to live out his baptismal call to love and bring Christ to the world. It is not a job, a hobby, a pastime, or even one of many important things a Christian might do. A vocation is meant to be our identity. It is intended to be our primary ministry. It is, ultimately, our path to fulfillment in Christ. Everything and everyone else can be allowed to share in our lives to the degree that they enable us to fulfill our vocations. St. Paul refers to everything that would distract him from his vocation as "a loss" or "much rubbish." Some translations use "dung" or "garbage to be thrown to the dogs" (see Phil 3:8). His point is not that work, hobbies, friends, and family are unimportant but that the expectations of the world—and the persecutions that inevitably come when we do not live up to those expectations—cannot be allowed to distract us from the unimaginable glory our vocation enables us to attain. To be free to be our true selves means that we have the ability to overcome the internal and external influences, distractions, and persecutions that seek to pull us away from fulfilling our vocational destiny. We have been given the power, by our heavenly Father, to bring his loving presence to our wives and children. There is no more important freedom we could be given than the ability to love and cherish our wives and children as God loves and cherishes them. We achieve this freedom in three ways:

1. Plugging into God's grace
2. Choosing mindfulness
3. Practicing your reactions

## 1. Plugging into God's grace

We must ask God every day for the courage to be men after his own heart. We must consciously ask God to make us more like him and to remind us—when we are tempted to give into others' demands to dance to their tunes—to stand firm in our faith, to be courageous, and to be strong as men of God are called to be (cf. 1 Cor 16:13).

When you wake up, dedicate your day to the Lord and ask him to remind you that you are, first and foremost, a husband and father after *the* Father's own heart. Pray that God would help you remember that, regardless of what else you may have to do, the most important task in your day is keeping your roles as husband and father before you. Ask God for the grace and wisdom you need to approach your work and every other obligation with your marriage and family life in mind with the intention of saving enough of yourself to give to your wife and children at the end of the day. Traditionally, this prayer is known as a "morning offering," and its intention is to help us dedicate every thought, word, and act to the service of our vocation and the greater glory of God. Doing this every morning helps set the stage for the second skill: practicing mindfulness.

## 2. Choosing mindfulness

Earlier we discussed how mindfulness can help you go deeper in your prayer life, but the benefits of this skill don't end there. It can also help us stand up to the resistance we encounter—both from within ourselves and from other people—when we are trying to put our marriages and family lives first.

Recall that being mindful is the opposite of being reactive. Mindfulness allows us to observe ourselves in the moment, pause before we act, and consciously choose to make the best response to a situation. Another word for mindfulness is what the theology of the body refers to as "receptivity"—that is, the ability to be open in every moment to the grace God wants to give us and to choose what he would have us do.

When we feel persecuted or criticized for anything, but especially for prioritizing our roles as husbands and fathers, our natural tendency is to react. For most of us, that means that we bend to the pressure of the moment and end up betraying our vocation. Mindfulness enables us to resist giving into the pressure of the moment and, instead, pause to think of how we might respond to the present challenge in a way that also enables us to attend to our other responsibilities. When we pray that God would help us remember to keep our vocation as husbands and fathers in the forefront of our minds, we plug into the power of God's grace.

Mindfulness, on the other hand, enables us to cooperate with the power of that grace throughout the day. If you have ever prayed for the grace to change something about yourself only to repeat that very same mistake several hours later, you have experienced how a lack of this quality impedes your ability to live in God's grace. Mindfulness is the cup that allows us to catch the outpouring of God's grace and carry it with us throughout the day so that we may take a drink when we are feeling parched and in danger of forgetting who we really are. It allows us to make the decision to leave work when it's time to go home instead of staying to answer "just one more e-mail"—only to look up three hours later. Mindfulness allows you to say, "I already have an appointment then," instead of agreeing to a business meeting at time that would cause you to miss your kid's school play. It enables us to tell our parents, friends, or other important people that, while we may not be available at the times they first propose, we are available to help or hang out at other times that don't cause us to shortchange our spouses and children.

There are many exercises we can use to practice mindfulness, but the simplest is to literally slow down our speech and actions. The less mindful we are, the quicker we act and the clumsier we are in word and deed. We say the wrong thing because we aren't pausing to consider the best thing to say. We spill our coffee all over our laptop because we aren't watching as we reach for the cup. We walk into the coffee table because we have allowed our minds to race ahead of us to the next room. In each of these instances, simply pausing a moment or slowing down enough to watch our actions (as our hand reaches for the cup or our feet cross the floor) enable us to remember who we are, where we are, and what the situation requires of us.

Pausing for a moment and/or slowing down our speech or actions when we feel attacked or criticized for prioritizing our wives and children gives our conscious minds the opportunity to catch up with our quicker, emotional brains and to redirect that energy into more productive responses.

### *3. Practicing your reactions*

Finally, we learn to respond more effectively to the persecutions that threaten our ability to put family first through practice. A colleague of mine likes to say, "Never underestimate your capacity to be surprised by the same damn thing happening over and over." No matter how many times we find ourselves pressured to put other people or responsibilities before our vocations as husbands and fathers, we are always surprised by it. Don't be. If you give into the pressure to throw your wife or kids under the bus because of someone else's disapproval, learn from the experience. Ask yourself afterward, "If I could have done this differently, how would I have responded?" If you don't know, talk it over with someone whose insights you respect. Write your answer down, and then bring your intention to act differently to God in your morning prayer. Imagine that, at some point during the day, you might experience a similar situation. Imagine yourself feeling tempted to respond by caving into the pressure or criticism, but then see yourself saying and doing the new thing. Conclude this exercise by asking God to help you remember this new opportunity to be faithful to your vocation and to help you use your mindfulness skills to carry your new resolution with you throughout the day.

Through prayer, mindfulness, and practice, you can learn to both resist and respond more effectively to the disapproval, criticism, and both real and imagined obstacles that are thrown in your path and that seek to stop you from being faithful to your vocation as husband and father. For your faithfulness, God will honor you with a place at the heavenly banquet.

## Questions for Reflection

- When do you feel pressured to put something or someone above your primary vocation of husband and father?
- If you were going to respond more faithfully in these situations, what would you need to do differently? How will you remember to be faithful to this resolution?
- How do you imagine praying to be faithful to your vocation, using mindfulness, and practicing alternatives can help you be more effective at resisting and responding to pressures to avoid putting your marriage and family first?

## Prayer

Heavenly Father, you let nothing stand between you and your children. At all times and in all seasons, you are always "Our Father." You have made me in your image. Help me to be faithful to my vocation to be the husband and father you want me to be, to resist the temptation to put anything before my wife and children, and to remain confident in my vocation despite the sacrifices it requires and the criticism it often entails. Make me faithful and steadfast, and help me count everything but the vocation you have given me as loss. Amen.

## *Blessed Are the Dads Who Are Persecuted*

### Your Relationship with Your Wife

Sometimes our attempts to be faithful husbands and fathers can, ironically, provoke persecution from our wives. Conventional Christian wisdom leads us to believe that every wife longs for a faithful, prayerful husband who lives to put his family first, but this is, unfortunately, not the case.

In my work, I encounter many men who, perhaps, had a conversion or reversion experience after they were married and had children. Sometimes this bears wonderful fruit on the home front, but just as often, wives can feel threatened by their husbands' newfound faith and can even be hostile or antagonistic when their husbands invite them to church, pray with the family, or even share their faith with the children.

Men who encounter this kind of hostility from their wives experience a special pain as their efforts to serve God and love their families are thrown back in their faces. In the face of such resistance and even anger, there is a strong temptation to turn one's faith into an entirely private or even secret enterprise. Men in this situation often feel that, because they cannot "make" their wives love God and the Church, they must simply keep their heads down "for the sake of the family" and hope that things will, somehow, change with time.

Sadly, this reaction tends to both prolong and sometimes even exacerbate the problem. There are several ways that a husband can respond gracefully to this situation:

1. Reframe the issue.
2. Love more generously.
3. Be patient and pray.

### *1. Reframe the issue.*

When faith becomes an issue in marriage, most people think that it is a religious problem. It is not. Many couples are not in the same place, spiritually speaking, and they manage their differences quite well. What really distinguishes couples who manage spiritual differences well from those who don't? Respect.

More than simply not trying to offend someone, respect represents the willingness to see the truth, goodness, and beauty in the things your mate finds true, good, and beautiful, especially when you don't naturally appreciate those things yourself. Respect for another person makes you say, "I love you, and I know you have a good head on your shoulders. If you like something, there must be something to appreciate about it. I don't have to love it as much as you do, but let me at least try to understand why it means so much to you so I can support you in it."

If your spouse responds to your efforts to practice and share your faith with hostility or antagonism, you will need to reframe the issue and insist that the problem be viewed as a failure of basic respect in the marriage, especially if you are have already been trying your best to be sensitive to the differences between the two of you.

It is true that you cannot make your wife and children love God and practice their faith to the same degree that you do, but you absolutely have a right to expect them to respect your faith and your attempts to—charitably and gently—share it with them. They should not merely tolerate it but join in it as they are able, appreciate it as they can, and, in particular, support you with all their heart. It is absolutely reasonable to expect an unchurched spouse to at least maintain a respectful, supportive silence when you lead family prayer (such as grace at meals); to come with you to church on Sundays as a sign of support to you and your children; to participate respectfully in conversation about your faith (including voicing respectful questions/concerns); and to encourage your children to participate fully in your efforts to share your faith with them. This is exactly how healthy, happy couples manage faith differences. If your nonbelieving wife does not respond to you this way, it is not because your faith is causing a problem in your marriage. It is because your marriage has a problem in it. Under such circumstances, it may be important for you to seek professional marital counseling to learn how to shore up the respect in your relationship. If you need additional support, contact the Pastoral Solutions Institute to learn about our tele-counseling services.

## *2. Love more generously.*

Especially if you are new convert/revert to your faith, it is natural for a nonbelieving spouse to feel a little insecure about your relationship with God. Chances are, your encounter with grace is changing you in ways that your wife is not sure how to cope with. Perhaps you have stopped doing things you used to enjoy together (for example, drinking/partying) because you realize they are not good for you. Perhaps you are discussing things that touch on uncomfortable subjects for her. Perhaps you are asking her to share in certain changes that she doesn't completely understand (for example, practicing NFP). Maybe she is afraid that you will become a person she doesn't know and can't like.

You can allay all of these concerns by becoming a more loving husband—the loving husband you never had the courage to be before your encounter with God's grace. One of the most common and most insidious problems in marriage is that husbands and wives tend to love their comfort zones more than they love each other. Our wives may ask us for many things, but we tend to do only those things that are comfortable for us. The rest we tend to forget or simply ignore. It is time for that to change. God pours out his love for you so abundantly. The best way to share that love with your wife—and show her that your faith is not something to be feared—is to begin to love her in all the ways that are meaningful to her, especially when those things challenge us to grow in ways that make us uncomfortable.

Make a list of all the things your wife has asked you to do for her over the years to show her that you love her but that you have tended to resist, reject, or ignore because they just "aren't your thing." Assuming that the things your wife has asked (is asking) of you are not objectively immoral, demeaning, or otherwise contrary to the practice of your faith, ask God for the grace and courage to do all of these things and more. Make a point of asking your wife—each day—what you can do to make her life easier or more pleasant. Let your faith be the source of a love and generosity toward your wife and children that she cannot help to be inspired and moved by.

If she asks you why you are being so nice to her, tell her that when you pray, you feel God's love for you and for her so much that it makes you want to share that love with her. If, inspired by your example, she asks what she can do for you, use that opportunity to ask her to either be more respectful of or join in some small way the practice of your faith. If she refuses, let it go. Continue to love without counting the cost. When you start to feel frustrated or resentful, take a hard look at the cross and remind yourself of all the times you refused to reciprocate God's love for you. Join your sufferings to the cross of Christ (see Col 1:24), and ask God to give you the strength to love your wife with all the passion, fervor, and commitment with which he loves you. The best way to evangelize to your spouse is not to preach, scold, or lecture. It is to love well, love better, and love more.

### *3. Be patient and pray.*

Especially when we are new to our faith, our fervor can sometimes make us blind to the way we come across to others. Without intending to, we can seem like we are criticizing, judging, or lecturing them. Assuming your wife is being generally respectful to you and your faith (as we discussed above), it can be helpful to acknowledge this possibility to your wife and give her permission to gently point it out to you.

This does not mean that your spouse has permission to tell you to not practice or share your faith openly in your home, with her, or with your children. Requests to stop going to church, stop praying with your kids, or stop discussing your spiritual life altogether should be understood, reframed, and dealt with as disrespect.

That said, it is a different matter to give your wife, who is generally respectful and supportive, the right to gently suggest that a change of topic might be in order or that you are coming on too strong in some way. Your willingness to give her permission to gently point out times when you get carried away will go a long way to helping her feel respected.

Of course, the most important thing to do is to pray, fast, and offer little sacrifices for the conversion of your wife's heart and the strength of your marriage. Don't pray that God would change your wife, though. Instead, pray that God would make you the man your wife needs you to be to inspire her to greater openness to his love and grace.

Ultimately, your mission is to be patient and supportive of her journey, whatever it is, to be as loving as your experience of God's grace empowers you to be, and to do all of this in the context of respecting her and expecting her to respect you in return.

This process can be challenging, and you may experience a great deal of what feels like persecution in your marriage. Through your willingness to be patient, loving, and respectful—and by working hard to foster a deepening of patience, love, and respect in your relationship—despite this sense of being persecuted, you will be able to both experience Christ's sacrifice in a more profound way in your life and share Christ's love in your home more generously. Be patient and trust that God's grace will be sufficient (see 2 Cor 12:9).

## Questions for Reflection

- When is it hardest for your wife to be supportive of your attempts to share or practice your faith at home or in general? Do you feel this struggle is more a sign of her disrespect for your spiritual journey or more an indication that you have been coming on too strong? How can you use the suggestions in this chapter to address this?
- What ways has your wife asked you to show love for her that you have tended to resist or ignore? How will you use your faith to help you practice greater courage and generosity in these areas?
- When is it hardest for you to be patient with your wife's spiritual progress (or lack thereof)? How would you like to respond to these situations more effectively in the future?

## Prayer

Heavenly Father, you love me faithfully, even when I am stubborn, unloving, and rejecting of your efforts to draw me closer to you. Help me to follow your example in my marriage. Make me the man my wife needs me to be, the man you would have me be, who is empowered, through your grace, to open his wife's heart to your love. Amen.

# *Blessed Are the Dads Who Are Persecuted*

## Your Relationship with Your Children

We want to give our children the best of everything. Christian fathers especially want to pass their faith on to their children. There is no greater gift a father can give his children than the ability to love and be loved by God.

When children are hostile or openly rejecting of the faith, Christian fathers experience immeasurable pain and frustration. It can be hard to know how to respond well to our kids' negative reactions to things such as church attendance, family prayer, or, even more significant, belief in God himself.

Many dads tend to respond to this negativity as an act of willful defiance. Understandably, we feel persecuted by our children's stubbornness and angered by the cavalier way they can throw faith both under the bus and back in our faces. Their rejection of our faith feels so personal because our faith is personal. Our faith defines us. It says who we are, what we hope, and in whom we hope.

Even so, faithful fathers do well not to see their children's faith struggles as acts of defiance but as ones of struggle or even pain. Here are some thoughts to keep in mind that can help you turn those times when you feel persecuted for your faith by your kids into opportunities to be blessed by God and to be a blessing to your children in turn:

1. Collect your kids.
2. Don't lecture; listen.
3. Make a plan together.
4. Pray.
5. Be strong.

### *1. Collect your kids.*

Although there are some exceptions, it is almost always true that the degree to which your child is antagonistic to your faith has less to do with his feelings about faith than it does his feelings about you. Our kids know how to hurt us, and when they themselves are hurting or angry enough, they will bring out the big guns to get our attention. A child's lack of motivation to pray, go to Mass, or believe in *the* Father at all often has to do with his feeling disconnected or alienated from his earthly father. New York University Professor Emeritus of Psychology Dr. Paul Vitz has observed that most atheists have terrible relationships with their fathers. Recall our discussion earlier about how the father is the "first other" to a child. On an unconscious level, the father represents what a child will need to live and succeed in "the world." When a child rejects your faith, he is really saying, "I don't want to live in your world. I want to get as far away from you as I can." The more antagonistic we are to our children in the face of their rebellions against our faith and values, the more we provide a ready justification for their behavior: "See? Your faith just makes you an angry jerk, and I don't want any part of that."

The first step in responding effectively to our children's defiance of our faith and values is to refuse to argue and instead focus on "collecting" our children.

Collecting the child involves making time to emotionally reconnect with a child. When we collect our children, we gently and lovingly say "come here" with our words and actions instead of "go away." Depending on the force of the defiance, collecting a child could be as simple as giving him a hug or an encouraging word or as complicated as getting a father-son weekend away. How much collecting you need to do directly depends on how much the child feels your relationship has fallen to pieces.

Recall our discussion on COAL. Remember that when you need to make a change in your life, your brain needs to be receptive to that change. Recall, further, that when you criticize yourself, your brain's ability to learn and change either becomes hampered or shuts down altogether. The brain responds to threats by redirecting energy from its potential to change and grow to its need to protect and stay put. The same is true for your children. The more they see you as the enemy—especially when it comes to issues of faith and morals—the more their brains shut down and they become reactive to anything you say or do. If you want to get their minds and hearts in a receptive place that is open to change and growth, you need to take down their emotional temperature by helping them feel that you love them and are on their side. It isn't enough to say it. They need to feel it. It requires real courage on your part, but learn to respond to any defiance—especially defiance about faith and values—by calming down, speaking gently, and making time to connect with and collect your child's heart. A small investment of time, love, and gentleness at the beginning of your discussions with your children will pay off big dividends in terms of their openness and receptivity to change when the process comes to an end.

## *2. Don't lecture; listen.*

Having collected your child, deepen the connection by listening first. We often respond to defiance about faith and values by lecturing. Our fear of losing our children's hearts and souls causes us to buy into the lie that the more we talk, the more effective we're being. The opposite is true.

Once you have gotten your child's emotional temperature down by collecting him, ask questions that get at the heart of why your child seems so angry or rejecting of God and the faith.

- What does this (going to Mass, praying, believing) mean to you? What makes it seem so hard/frustrating/undesirable/etc.?
- I get the impression that you feel like this (God/the Church/faith) is making your life harder or more frustrating somehow. Can you help me understand why?
- Do you feel like faith is somehow making it harder for you to handle some personal situation/deal with a relationship with a friend/meet some need or desire?

- Do you feel like God is real to you? Or do you tend to just go through the motions because it's what I've told you to do?

My wife and I go into much more detail about how to both ask and respond to these kinds of questions in *Discovering God Together: The Catholic Guide to Raising Faithful Kids.* The point here is to make sure that you respond to your child's antagonism about faith matters in a manner that says, "I hear the message you are sending me underneath all the anger and defiance, and I want to hear what you are really trying to say to me. Let's talk. I'm listening."

### *3. Make a plan together.*

Once you understand the nature of your child's hostility to church, your faith, or your values, make a plan together. If your child is frustrated because your rules or expectations are making it hard for him to meet some need or accomplish some goal, use the "positive opposite technique" we discussed in an earlier chapter to help your child achieve that goal in a godly manner. If your child feels that your faith somehow means that he has to judge, criticize, or otherwise degrade someone who isn't living according to Christian values, help him understand how it is possible to disagree with someone but still love that person. If your child feels that he has never had a real experience of God and that church is just a bunch of empty rituals, work together to figure out how to help your child make that personal connection.

Again, it is beyond the scope of this book to solve these particular problems. *Discovering God Together* can help you form effective responses to these challenges and more. The takeaway, for now, is to respond to your child's concerns or objections not by explaining them away or telling him to "get over it" but rather by making a plan that helps him experience his faith as a resource rather than a burden.

## *4. Pray.*

By all means, pray for your children, but don't just pray *for* them. Pray with them and pray over them. Don't ask permission. Just do it. Put up with the eye-rolls. Let the snide comments roll off your back. Right in the moment, ask God to help you be the father your child needs you to be, to open your heart to your child's needs, and to help your child receive all the gifts God wants to give him. Resist the temptation to lecture through your prayers ("God, please make my child stop being so defiant and rebellious!"). Model how to use prayer as an honest request for grace and assistance with the problem at hand ("God, help me be sensitive to my son's needs, and help us figure out a plan together for now to solve this tough problem he's facinging").

Children and teens need to see that prayer is personal and powerful. If they see you "saying prayers" but don't witness how prayer can facilitate their personal encounters with God and give them powerful ways to respond to the challenges in their lives, they will write off prayer as just so many empty words. Make prayer a part of your conversations and problem-solving discussions with your kids. Even if they won't pray with you, let them see that prayer is the source of your support, love, and commitment to them. Let them witness the difference that prayer makes in their relationship with you, and, when they are ready, show them how they can make their own connections with God.

## *5. Be strong.*

As we discussed earlier in this book, meekness is not weakness. Adopting an open, listening, helpful response does not mean accepting poor treatment from your children or lowering your standards.

If, despite your best efforts to respond sensitively to your child, he treats you with disrespect, it is more than OK to apply simple consequences—like time-outs, for instance—that require him to calm down and figure out how to continue the conversation in a respectful way. Likewise, being willing to help your child find godly ways to meet his needs to gain appropriate freedoms or build healthy social connections does not mean you are willing to surrender your moral standards so that your child will like you or so that you can be your child's best friend. Be generous. Be helpful. But be clear that, while you will move heaven and earth to help your child get his needs met in godly ways, you will not support his pursuit of any goals that are destructive, immoral, or unhealthy. Let your children know that you love them enough to insist on the best from them and the best for them.

The more you are able to respond to your children's attempts to persecute you for your efforts to raise them in faithful ways, the more likely it is that you will be able to diffuse your children's anger and open their hearts to the movement of God's grace.

Jesus says that those who are persecuted for the sake of righteousness will inherit the kingdom of heaven. Let this promise be your consolation whenever you are persecuted for your efforts to establish, maintain, or lead a godly household.

## Questions for Reflection

- How does the approach described in this chapter differ from the way you usually respond to your children's objections to/criticisms of your attempts to live your faith at home? What difference would it make in your home to use the suggestions in this chapter?
- What is the nature of your children's criticisms of your faith and/or your attempts to form them in the faith?
- How can you work with your children to offer godly ways to meet the needs that serve as the source of their antagonism or resentment toward your faith?

## Prayer

Heavenly Father, my children are your greatest gift to me, but they can also be the source of my greatest heartache. Help me to see their objections, criticisms, and even rejections of my faith as an opportunity to minister more effectively to their hurts, help them meet their needs, and lead them to you through gentle, loving means. Give me the heart of a shepherd, and help me bring my sheep home to you. Amen.

# CONCLUSION

## A Father's Love

Pope Francis asserted that the Beatitudes are the pattern of the Christian life. Throughout this book, it has been my goal to help you see the radical difference Jesus' eight principles of Christian discipleship can make in your fathering ministry. God himself has invited us to walk these stepping stones to wholeness and holiness. Reflecting upon the path the Beatitudes lay out in light of our fatherhood enables us to draw closer to God and bear witness to the world in three critical, life-altering ways.

First, it enables us to experience the love of our heavenly Father more personally, more deeply, and more meaningfully. Our encounter with that love enables us to be men after the Father's own heart.

Next, it helps us transform our relationships with our wives—the mothers of our children—so that we can experience the free, total, faithful, and fruitful love that comes from the Father's own heart and can give the world a concrete encounter with the love that everyone longs for.

Finally, it helps us bring the Father's face to our children by enabling us to love them in ways that help them become everything they were created to be and draw close to the heart of their Father in heaven, who is the source of every good gift.

Seen in this manner, fatherhood is not just a role we play. It isn't just a job we do. It is, as St. John Paul II asserted, the fullest expression of our vocation as men and the most important way we can cooperate with God's plan for our lives. It is our path to holiness. It is our path to fulfillment. It is our path to healing. And it is our path to joy.

Every man wants to leave a mark on the world, to leave a legacy. Sadly, many men sacrifice their fatherly vocation pursuing generativity by means that will be forgotten within a few years, if not days or weeks, after they are gone from this earth. But a father will always be remembered for the impact he has had on his family. Even if future generations fail to recall his name, his impact and presence will continue to be felt—for good or for ill—in the minds, hearts, and spirits of his children and his children's children. There is no greater way to impact future generations for the greater glory of God than to be the best father you can be, the father your wife and children need you to be, the father God is calling you to be. Each of the BeDADitudes is an invitation to go deeper, to become love incarnate—just as Christ is love incarnate—in your home.

Most people are familiar with the passage from 1 Corinthians 13 (vv. 1–12) that describes how Christians are called to love one another. Most of us think of this as a wedding passage, but as Pope Francis reminds us in *The Joy of Love*, it is more than that. It is a passage that ultimately describes the kind of love that the heavenly Father has for each of us, his children. Seen in the context of the eight BeDADitudes, this passage describes the kind of love that God expects each of us earthly fathers to model in our homes. Imagine how this famous passage describes the heavenly Father's own heart and, as such, serves as a model for each Christian father:

> If I speak in the tongues of men or of angels, but I am not a loving father, I am only a resounding gong or a clanging cymbal. If I have the gift of prophecy and can fathom all

> mysteries and all knowledge, and if I have a faith that can move mountains, but am not a loving father, I am nothing. If I give all I possess to the poor and give over my body to hardship that I may boast, but I am not a loving father, I gain nothing. A loving father is patient, a loving father is kind. He does not envy, he does not boast, he is not proud. He does not dishonor others, he is not self-seeking, he is not easily angered, he keeps no record of wrongs. A loving father does not delight in evil but rejoices with the truth. He always protects, always trusts, always hopes, always perseveres. A father's love never fails. But where there are prophecies, they will cease; where there are tongues, they will be stilled; where there is knowledge, it will pass away. For we know in part and we prophesy in part, but when completeness comes, what is in part disappears. When I was a child, I talked like a child, I thought like a child, I reasoned like a child. When I became a father, I put the ways of childhood behind me. For now we see only a reflection as in a mirror; then we shall see the Father face to face. (see 1 Cor 13:1–12)

This vision of fatherhood is as intimidating as it is awe-inspiring, but it is exactly the kind of love that every Christian father is called to give to his wife and children.

The eight BeDADitudes serve as the map to living out this love in the heart of your home. Do you want to make your mark on the world? Do you wish for your name to be praised for generations to come? Do you want your children, your children's children, and their children to know God more fully because of the man you were today? At the end of your life, do you want to hear, "Well done, my good and faithful servant!"?

If you have answered "yes" to any of these questions, then I challenge you to join me in practicing the eight BeDADitudes each day for the rest of your days. Yes, we will struggle. Yes, we will stumble. In the words of G. K. Chesterton, "Anything worth doing is worth doing badly." But with God's grace, despite our imperfections and struggles we will run the race. We will be victorious. We will win the crown.

We will be fathers after the Father's own heart. And our houses will serve the Lord.

# A MESSAGE FROM THE AUTHOR

Dear Reader,
I hope you have been inspired by the eight BeDADitudes to see your fatherhood in a powerful new light.

We all do our best to be the men we are called to be, but sometimes we need a little help along the way. If you find that you are struggling in your efforts to be the father you would like to be, the father your wife and children need you to be, the father God is calling you to be, I invite you to contact the Pastoral Solutions Institute (PSI) to learn more about both our spiritual direction counseling and tele-counseling services.

Through both of these unique programs, we at PSI help couples, families, and individuals around the world live more joyful, grace-filled lives. Our professional spiritual directors and counselors are licensed at the highest levels, faithful to the Church, and specially trained to integrate the insights of our Catholic faith with cutting-edge psychological techniques to help you achieve your goals for your personal, married, and family life.

If you would like additional support in becoming a man after God's own heart, contact the Pastoral Solutions Institute today at 740-266-6461, or visit www.catholiccounselors.com, and discover how we can help you overcome the obstacles that stand between you and the man you were meant to be.

Yours in Christ,
Dr. Greg Popcak

# NOTES

1. Francis, "The Beatitudes: A Practical Program for Holiness," Vatican Radio, http://en.radiovaticana.va/news/2014/06/09/pope_the_beatitudes,_a_practical_programme_for_holiness/1101553 (accessed November 22, 2016).

2. Francis, "The Beatitudes: A Practical Program for Holiness," Vatican Radio, https://zenit.org/articles/pope-s-morning-hom-ily-beatitudes-are-practical-programme-for-holiness/ (accessed November 22, 2016).

3. Linda Hatch, "Why Isn't Married Sex Hot?" Psych Central, http://blogs.psychcentral.com/sex-addiction/2016/05/why-isnt-married-sex-hot/ (accessed November 22, 2016).

4. Susan Ratcliffe, ed., *Oxford Essential Quotations* (Oxford: Oxford University Press, 2015), http://www.oxfordreference.com/view/10.1093/acref/9780191804144.001.0001/q-oro-ed3-00010592?result=7&rskey=xMAN9J (Accessed November 22, 2016).

More Titles by Dr. Greg Popcak

## MARRIAGE

For Better FOREVER (with Lisa Popcak)
Just Married (with Lisa Popcak)
Holy Sex!
When Divorce Is Not an Option
A Marriage Made for Heaven (with Lisa Popcak)
Living a Joy-Filled Marriage (with Tom McCabe)

## PARENTING & FAMILY LIFE

Parenting with Grace (with Lisa Popcak)
Beyond the Birds and the Bees (with Lisa Popcak)
Discovering God Together (with Lisa Popcak)
The Corporal Works of Mommy (and Daddy Too) (with Lisa Popcak)
Then Comes Baby (with Lisa Popcak)

## CHRISTIAN LIVING

Broken Gods
The Life God Wants You to Have
God Help Me! These People Are Driving Me Nuts
God Help Me! This Stress Is Driving Me Crazy

**Gregory K. Popcak** is a psychotherapist, the executive director of Pastoral Solutions Institute, and the author of more than twenty popular books and programs integrating Catholic theology and counseling psychology. He is an expert on the practical applications of the theology of the body. His books include *Just Married*, *Then Comes Baby*, and *Parenting with Grace*. He is a regular contributor to *Catholic Digest*, *Family Foundations*, and other magazines. He hosts *More2Life* with his wife, Lisa, on Ave Maria Radio. The couple have three children and live in Ohio.

Founded in 1865, Ave Maria Press, a ministry of the Congregation of Holy Cross, is a Catholic publishing company that serves the spiritual and formative needs of the Church and its schools, institutions, and ministers; Christian individuals and families; and others seeking spiritual nourishment.

For a complete listing of titles from

Ave Maria Press

Sorin Books

Forest of Peace

Christian Classics

visit www.avemariapress.com